DEAD AND FAT CATS

A NO-NONSENSE JOURNEY THROUGH OUR DYSFUNCTIONAL FISHING INDUSTRY

Eric Wickham

Foreword by Dr. David Suzuki

National Library of Canada Cataloguing in Publication

Wickham, Eric, 1942-
Dead fish and fat cats : a no-nonsense journey through
our dysfunctional fishing industry / Eric Wickham.

ISBN 1-894694-18-X

1. Pacific salmon fisheries--Canada.
2. Fishery management--Canada.
3. Wickham, Eric, 1942-.
4. Fishers--Canada--Pacific Coast--Biography.
I. Title.

SH349.W52 2002   338.3'72756'09711   C2002-904014-0

Cover and book design: Fiona Raven
Copy editing: Neall Calvert
Front cover cat illustration: Teresa Waclawik
Front cover fish illustration: Annie Branley / Optima Printing
Back cover photograph: Steve Bosch / Vancouver Sun

First Printing January 2003
Printed in Canada

Granville Island
Publishing

Suite 212–1656 Duranleau
Vancouver, BC, Canada V6H 3S4
Tel 604-688-0320 Toll-free 1-877-688-0320
www.granvilleislandpublishing.com

Contents

Dedicated

to my
three wonderful daughters
Andrea, Sara and Britta

Acknowledgments

I would like to thank Jim Heath for all his assistance and introducing his wonderful sense of humour to the book, Tom Simons for spending years encouraging me to write it, Bob Alfort and John Sanderson for their valuable suggestions, and the team at Granville Island Publishing: publisher and managing editor Jo Blackmore, designer Fiona Raven, and copy editor Neall Calvert.

Foreword

by Dr. David Suzuki

When I wrote my autobiography, *Metamorphosis: Stages in a Life*, the reviewer for the *Globe and Mail* commented that, judging from the pictures and number of references, I obviously loved fish more than my first wife. My earliest memories of childhood all revolve around fishing, hiking and camping. That's where I learned my most important biology lessons, and for years I yearned to be a fish biologist.

I remember accompanying my dad in the late 1930s to jig for halibut off Spanish Banks in Vancouver, troll for sea-run cutthroats around Stanley Park, catch sturgeon in the Fraser and hike up the Vedder River for steelhead and Dolly Varden. Those were some of the happiest and most formative times in my life.

Today fishing remains in the family blood and my grandchildren often call, begging to be taken fishing. But there's no way I could take them to experience what I did as a child, because the fish are gone. Within the lifetimes of my own children, I've watched once plentiful and huge ling and rock cod disappear, abundant herring decline drastically, the Vancouver Sun Salmon Derby cancelled for lack of salmon, abalone vanish. Even youngsters today will tell us, "Oh yes, I remember when there used to be a creek over there" or "I remember when I used to go fishing with Dad for _____ (fill in the blank)."

"There used to be" is a phrase that fills me with sadness, and

I hear it often, everywhere I go. The tragedy of what is playing out on our coasts is about far more than economics, politics or jobs. It's about community and spirit, a reflection of the loss of balance with nature, a confused sense of place and belonging. In our relentless, shortsighted attempt to maximize profit or gain political points, we try to put nature on steroids, pump up trees, fish or birds to fulfill human priorities and demands.

As a broadcaster and journalist, I have reported on countless species and ecosystems around the world that are in trouble. And everywhere I am amazed at the human capacity to rationalize away responsibility by finding convenient scapegoats, from voracious seals to foreign fishing fleets to El Niños. But consider this: We don't know enough to manage anything out there in the real world. Hell, we don't even have an inventory of all the species there are in the world, let alone a blueprint informing us how the components are all interlinked.

The eminent Harvard biologist Edward O. Wilson estimates that we may have identified (i.e., given a scientific name to a dead specimen) 10–15 percent of all animal and plant species in the world. Of these, we know the life cycle, geographic range and ecological role of less than 0.1 percent in some detail. At some point, we have to confront that image reflected from the mirror and begin to accept some responsibility, whether by the way we work, play, or consume. After all, human beings are the only component that we have any hope of controlling and managing.

Long after I graduated with a PhD and had become a university professor, my father would point out that I was behaving like "an educated fool." With all of the books, fancy lingo, labs and equipment, I often lacked simple "common sense." "Look around, for heaven's sake, can't you see? It's obvious," Dad would often exclaim in exasperation. And he was always right. He was my greatest mentor and teacher, and even today I think of him and try to keep it clear and simple and to filter out the bullshit.

Eric Wickham must have had a dad like mine. His delightful book has an effective B.S. filter tightly in place. He tells it like it is; he's unflinchingly honest, wickedly funny and on-target insightful. As an experienced and aging (sorry, Eric, but you're becoming an elder) commercial fisherman, he has lived through the catastrophic decline of marine fish and the consequent impact on people and communities that depend on fishing.

I have long felt that the fate of salmon and other marine "resources" reflects criminal action or inaction and that people should have been put in the slammer. Wickham's reflections are right on target. They ought to be read by everyone who cares about finding a harmonious way for humans to live with the rest of creation.

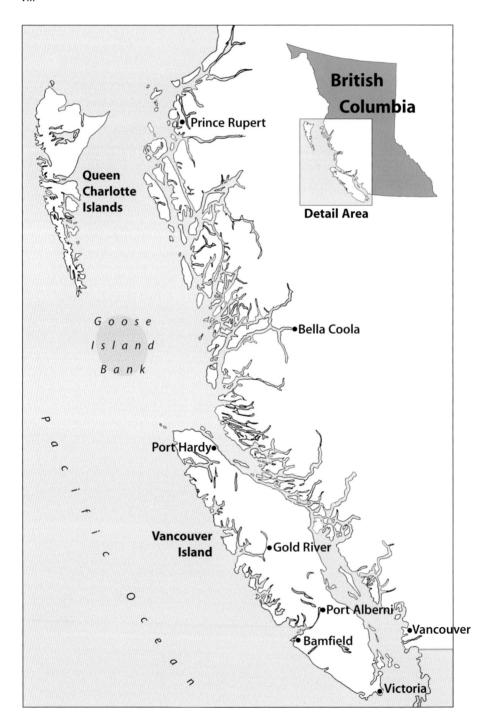

British Columbia

Detail Area

Prince Rupert

Queen Charlotte Islands

Goose Island Bank

Bella Coola

Port Hardy

Pacific Ocean

Vancouver Island

Gold River

Port Alberni

Vancouver

Bamfield

Victoria

1

How I *used to* catch salmon

Regard me at 22: tall, with well-developed muscles, and a squarish and honest face that would have seemed right for the hero in an old Western. Not to say lusty and hard-drinking. But I knew about fish, not cattle. I was already a deck hand on my dad's seagoing boat the summer I was a mere eight. Nature had also wired part of my brain for business. But those commercial capacities didn't strike me — or anyone else — until much later. They weren't visible in the fishing village where I grew up.

At 22, what sort of things did I *not* know? Not enough about women's *minds*. But I'm not going to say much about women. This book is about fish.

Here's another thing I didn't know at 22: what was developing in the Canadian fishing industry. In the political depths. Because salmon were easy to catch, I had moved out of the village and had my own boat. If there was any fish problem looming, I didn't detect it.

There were many other things I didn't know. I'll get to them. This is a tale of bouncy optimism, rude setbacks, gradual awakening, increasing prosperity, fishing discoveries, melancholy interludes, and even a shipwreck.

But now consider my first boat — *Joy II*. It cost me $7,000, and carried a mortgage of $5,000. I paid a $2,000 deposit from savings I'd earned by crewing on other people's boats. After high school I crewed full time for three years, mainly for my older brother Henry.

My first boat had a mild curse on it. I heard about it from the insurance auditor, who said: "For $7,000 you're buying $10,000 worth of trouble." I ignored him.

Now behold the boat itself. It's 32 feet long (which means it would fit into your living room, if you have a spacious one). There's a cabin, where I can sleep and keep out of the weather. There's a refrigerator for some of my food supplies — I take food for a week. There's a fibreglass fish-hold, kept cold with crushed ice. That's for the dead salmon.

I navigate by magnetic compass (this was 1964). A depth-sounder tells me how deep the bottom is. But it doesn't alert me

Joy II gets a clean-up.

to schools of fish, the way every normal sonar would a decade later.

I run this boat myself. I do everything. No crew — anyway, there's no room for them.

Let's go fishing.

It's a June day, four o'clock in the morning. The boat is anchored 40 miles off the rugged, forested, almost unpopulated Canadian coast. The captain of the vessel lies asleep in his cabin. He may snore sometimes, but I don't know, because it's me. In any case, he sleeps well. Yesterday the catch was OK; the weather is holding, and there's the lap, lap, lap of the water against the hull, measuring time peacefully.

BRRRRRRRING! The alarm clock. Outside it's dark, but the first grim light of dawn shows in the east. (The dawn may soon expand into a masterpiece, one of those "rosy-fingered" dawns that Homer reports on in *The Odyssey*.) My purpose in getting out of bed is to be up before the salmon. Motivation for this is easy to find, because of the mortgage on the boat.

I make coffee and a goodly breakfast, using a dark stove that burns diesel fuel. I brush my teeth, but I *don't* have a shower. I *never* have a shower. The boat carries 30 gallons of fresh water that has to last a week.

It has grown lighter outside. I can see the outlines of other boats anchored here and there. Their lights are still on — we all leave our lights on at night, to warn freighters. We see them passing, portholes glowing faintly, like many-eyed monsters. When there's fog, we anchor our boats close, hoping that our lights might combine to give more oomph.

We have all anchored on the same "bank" — a flat area underwater, very spacious, that's raised above the seabed like a gigantic submerged mesa. These banks attract fish. The fish seem to feed well there. I don't know why.

I venture out on deck. I'm wearing as much wool as four sheep. (It's June, but this is offshore Canada.) I am snug in thick wool pants, a heavy wool coat, not to mention wool underwear. I pull down my red wool hat until it covers my eyebrows. There's a light wind, but chill, maybe five knots, and a strong swell. The air, as you'd expect, smells fresh and salty. A few seagulls wheel around, as if they know what's coming.

I start the electric winch to raise the anchor. The seabed lies 200 feet down and the anchor surfaces about a minute later.

Then I push a red button on the diesel engine. ("Dark was that day when Rudolf Diesel conceived his grim engine.") Some black smoke puffs out. What do you expect — there's fire in this engine! It's a six-cylinder that puts out 80 horsepower. I am the first to start up this morning, though I see figures moving around on other boats.

I bring *Joy II* up to 2 knots (2.3 miles per hour). I've already worked out a course by considering the wave direction (I want to run into the waves or ride with them), but maybe have to compromise a bit to stay on the good fish runs. Soon the other boats will get moving, and we may need to talk, so we can run in parallel courses. Otherwise we'd spend our time dodging each other.

I steer to the course I want, then lock it with the autopilot — a control system that's one of *Joy II*'s rarest devices: something that hasn't been repaired by any of the boat's former owners. It therefore works flawlessly. Bless that thing! At the end of every run across the bank, I steer the boat around 180 degrees and lock it onto its new course, back in the opposite direction.

Two long fishing poles are mounted on the deck. They lean out over the water, one on each side of the boat. These aren't ordinary sports-fishing poles. These are money-making poles that carry three lines each and many hooks on each line.

My next mission is to get all six fishing lines into the water. This takes about half an hour. It doesn't take all that time because

I'm slothful. The reasons are more involved. Each line is 180 feet long and wound onto its own "gurdy" — a large bronze spool. The fishing line is stainless steel, about half as thick as coat-hanger wire (and very flexible). To let out a line, I push a lever on its gurdy. The lever engages a belt that's running all the time on the boat's motor. Out goes the line, at a controlled pace. But the first

The wild, solitary fish catcher.

thing into the water is a 50-pound lead weight on the end of the line. The speed of the boat keeps this weight from sinking too far. The weight drags the line behind the boat, at an angle. As the line keeps unwinding, I snap on hooks. Actually it's a hook-module: a short length of line (a leader), then a hook and a lure. Snap! Pause. Snap! Pause. Every 20 feet of line that goes by, there's a mark. That's where I snap on a hook. Seven hooks per line. (Just seven! A few years later I'd put on more than a hundred! But in the period I'm talking about now, fishermen* "knew" that too many hooks would scare the fish.)

I'm telling you these details for two reasons: (1) You may have an inquisitive, probing, restlessly technical, all-absorbing brain and demand to know; and (2) It will begin to illustrate that commercial fishing is not exactly a holiday. Also, that I'd better be paying close attention during this hook-snapping operation, because the hooks are more than two inches long and sharp as scalpels.

Right, the lines are out. Forty-two hooks in all. I'm cruising along slowly, hooks coursing through the water, lures dancing around them. Maybe you think I've overlooked something? The engine noise! Won't it scare the fish? No. Well, it *might*, if I had a decrepit engine that went BANG, BANG, BANG. If I had *anything* in the boat that made a repetitive BANG, BANG, that might ruin my fishing. That sound does scare fish.

Some fishermen go further. I've been cornered in pubs by old hands who advised me that fish are *attracted* to a smooth-running engine. The musical throb of the pistons, the propeller swishing pleasantly like some giant mother fish — pure fish enchantment. Uh-huh. Right. Very interesting. To test this proposition, someone would have to cruise along in a noiseless boat (a sailboat?) at the same speed, fishing in the same water, using the same lures and so on. Which has never been tried with scientific severity. Or at all, probably.

Anyway, I'm at least not scaring away fish. Now what happens?

Winching in the fish

Each line has a bell on it. It's right at the top of the pole: there's

---

* The term "fisherman" is used throughout this book to describe those of both sexes. I felt that using the politically correct term "fisher" would be inappropriate. I checked with three women who fish full time, and they were all proud to be called "fisherman."

a spring, which acts as a shock absorber for hot-tempered fish that yank unnaturally hard, then there's the bell, then the start of the fish line. When a fish gets hooked, I hear the bell. It's so loud it could probably be used as the doorbell for a castle.

OK, all six lines are out. Time passes. More time. Then, hey! Hear that bell? At least *one* fish has been caught *somewhere* on that line. Maybe just one fish and it might be on the *last* hook at the end of the line. Never mind, it's a catch and I bring it in. So I engage the gurdy again, but in reverse gear so it winds the line back in. I unclip each swinging, dripping, and empty hook as it goes by. (If I left the empty hooks on, imagine what would happen when they got to the gurdy.)

I stop the gurdy. Thump. There in the water thrashes a captive salmon. It probably weighs eight pounds. I don't try to haul it in on the line, because salmon have weak mouths. The hook might pull out. Instead I grab a gaff — a pole with a sharp hook on the end. I impale the flapping and fighting fish with this implement of yore, get it on deck, and whack the active creature on the head with a club until it stops moving. I don't want it flapping and scraping off its scales. These fish need to *look* good at the market. I then extract both the fishhook and the gaff, as blood leaks from the fish. (Some people don't like to hear this. But hey, this is where your fish come from.)

Before I gut and freeze this fish, let me reveal more fishing theory. You may wonder — or wordlessly sense — that there's something peculiar about going to the trouble of running out a line with seven hooks on it (in later years, 100-plus hooks), and then just hauling in *one* fish. Why not use a line with only one hook, and save work?

Answer: using many hooks increases the statistical odds in the fisherman's favour. The fish swim this way and that, seemingly at random. With a lot of hooks spread out in the water, the chances increase that *some* fish will encounter *some* lure. Also, if the fish are biting well, I may haul in many fish at once. Which happens.

That statistical advantage compensates for dealing with all those hooks and lures, snapping them on and off. That activity is not a lot of fun, it is always hazardous (ow! fuck!), and also leads to a perturbed mind when the removed hooks get tangled. A gust of wind, and all the hooks laid out on deck in precise rows might suddenly blow into a snarled hook-heap.

Gutting and packing

Picture me now, with that new-killed salmon. One fish! All this gear and the boat, all this fuss, and here's *one* fish! At that time, when I was 22, none of this struck me as odd. It was how I grew up. Fish very often came off long lines of hooks in *ones*. Obviously.

I must gut the fish and clean it right away. I use a fish knife — a very sharp item, with a fairly short blade. The back of it has a thing that looks like a spoon. That's used for cleaning the fish, scooping out the gooey parts that you want to get rid of. The scrapings go into a trough, where there's always water running. Swoosh — overboard (as seagulls dive and fight). It all needs to be done fast, while the fish is still bleeding. Then it bleeds itself. This improves the market quality of its meat.

Swinging open a horizontal hatch, with the gutted fish in one hand, I descend into the fish-hold. Down there, the ceiling is too low for me to stand up. A single light bulb illuminates this salmon mortuary. There are six "pens" — partitioned areas, packed with crushed ice. The place isn't refrigerated, but it's well-insulated. There's also a feeble cooling unit, about the size of a car's air-conditioner. It doesn't qualify as refrigeration, but it's some help. It extracts part of the heat that burrows through the insulation during a week at sea.

Each fish gets the same care: I stuff ice in its belly, lay it on top of the pen I'm filling, and cover it with a shroud of ice.

Back on deck, I wait for another bell. I may wait all day. (The logbook groans about days when I caught exactly one fish.) Or maybe I wait just five minutes and have many bells sound, all about the same time. This gets me moving like a hyperactive gymnast.

From rosy-fingered dawn to black night

In the lulls, and there can be many, I can reflect on anything I want to consider. I don't — at 22 — frown and struggle with questions like "What does it all mean?" or "Did this intricately meshing universe arise by chance or is it a Grand Design?" No. The questions are more like: "How come I never catch any herring?"

The abstract and generalized herring question became: "Why are lures so specific?" It seemed weird. I was beating a watery path back and forth over areas that were overcrowded cities of fish. There were herring, hake, halibut, several sorts of salmon, cod and even skipjack tuna. Sometimes they flapped and frolicked on the surface, in exuberance or defiance — catch me if you can! But it was so rare to catch anything but chinook or coho salmon that such an event called for an entry in the boat's logbook.

Consider the sockeye salmon. Delicious and valuable, as river fishermen knew, but it seemed immune to capture using our deep-sea methods. Thousands of hooks and lures were passing by, but the schools of sockeye ignored them all. Tons of fish, protected by some force field. Fishermen elevated this to a law of nature: *It Is Impossible to Catch Sockeye on Hook and Line.*

Eight years later, it was found that by changing the colour of a certain lure to red, making the lures smaller, and dragging them more slowly through the water (and only in certain directions!), anyone could catch sockeye like crazy. And guess what? No *other* fish would take those lures.

Fishing is a kind of key-and-lock business. One key opens one lock. Each key is useless for other locks. And there's no master key (no single lure catches every kind of fish). Very little of this was understood by me or anyone else in those days, as I cruised along in *Joy II*.

All day I was either hauling in fish, or packing them, or looking after the boat. Or *thinking* about fishing, or talking about fishing over the radiophone. For the record, here's a typical conversation between me and Charlie (let's say) in a nearby boat:

What was said:	What was meant:
Me: "Humpback, are you on here, Charlie? It's *Joy II*."	"Humpback" is Charlie's boat. This was an open channel, like CB radio. Anyone in range could talk or listen in.
Charlie: "Yeah, Eric. How are you doing? You catching anything?"	Standard opening: "You catching anything?"
Me: "No, no. I'm not getting anything. I got a few yester-day. How are you doing?"	*Never* admit you're doing well. But always mention some fish from "yesterday." That covers you when you land with fish in your hold.
Charlie: "Well, we're getting the odd one here. If you're getting nothing there, you might want to come here."	Charlie is doing really well, but he'll never say so. Yet he's willing to give me this hint.
Me: "I'll maybe just hang out here, and see if something happens."	That's me thanking Charlie, but letting him know I'm doing just fine too.

The conversations were low key. I can't remember a single upbeat example, even when everyone's boat was practically sinking under the weight of its fish load.

The only OK conversation was about fishing. Wives and girlfriends weren't talked about, except when they connected to fish. ("Tanya always overcooks pollack.") Politics weren't discussed, but maybe should have been, considering what politicians later did to fishing — and were doing then, almost unnoticed. Sports and cars weren't mentioned.

First catch of the day.

That's what one day's fishing was like. Up at 4 a.m., stop about 10:30 p.m. By then it was inky night, usually cloudy; the boats were running with lights on. We fished more than 18 hours.

Finally to sleep. Far gone in weariness.

If you mentally replay that day seven times, you get a picture of my typical fishing trip. By the end of a week, I was low on fresh water, food and diesel. But I'd have maybe 2,500 pounds of salmon in the hold. The most I ever caught was about 5,000 pounds. That was rare.

Here are some numbers. I'd spent 18-plus hours a day fishing. Allowing for travel to and from the fishing banks, I'd put in something like 115 fishing hours in a week. To end up with 2,500 pounds of fish, I'd need to catch an average of 22 pounds of fish an hour. A salmon weighs 6-8 pounds, say 7 pounds average. So I'd need to average about 3 fish per hour, or a fish every 20 minutes.

That's the sort of data that ends up in the federal Department of Fisheries and Ocean's data bank: "A 32-foot salmon boat catches an average of one salmon every 20 minutes." A bureaucratic factoid. A multitude of such fishing statistics are drawn together into a Picasso-like picture of fishing, with the parts in strange places and everything distorted. Some people at the Department might even imagine a fisherman sitting at a kind of seafaring desk — bolted to the deck — with a line overboard. Every 20 minutes, a fish bites and is hauled in.

The Department of Fisheries and Oceans has played a grave role in Canada's fishing-collapse drama. In ancient Greek dramas, similar wreckage was caused by the goddess Nemesis. She had a knack for spotting undeserved happiness and punishing it. But Nemesis definitely *knew what she was doing*. So the comparison with the Department of Fisheries and Oceans is weak here.

Selling them before the ice melts

Back to the point of my week-long salmon hunt: how much was 2,500 pounds of salmon worth in those days? I don't have records for individual catches, but I grossed $9,200 in my first season. Dividing $9,200 by 26 weeks (the length of the season) gives an average fish-value per trip of $354. On that I was able to live while fishing, pay for running the boat, survive during the off-season, fix up the boat, and pay off part of my $5,000 loan. (In two years I'd pay off the whole loan.)

Picture me now at the end of a week, my boat pregnant and encumbered with ice-packed cargo. The ice isn't melting, but it won't last too long. As already noted, I'm almost out of food and water. So I can't cruise up and down the Canadian coast, getting bids for my fish. No way! I head for the nearest coastal "buying station." These stations were set up jointly by fish-processing groups, to make it easy for fishermen to sell into the fresh-fish market — where the best prices are found. The fish bought by the stations go right to one of the big fresh-fish processors in Vancouver. Always by road, in refrigerated trucks, and quickly.

Canneries bought fish too, but they paid much less. Fish that gets sealed into cans doesn't have to look wonderful. No one notices some missing scales or other blemishes. I'll get to the canneries later, especially when I scowl about the fish-farm delusion.

So I'm now heading almost due east toward Bamfield. It's a buying station I often use, a town on the west coast of Vancouver Island. I'm forty miles out, so I can't actually *see* Bamfield. I can't see anything but wine-dark sea. Forty miles is way over the horizon (and it feels like a thousand miles, if a storm rises.)

The diesel pluckily pushes me landward. But not fast — the trip takes five hours. Meanwhile, there's nothing much to do. I talk to the guys by radio and tidy up the boat. I may wash dishes (using salt water). The 357 dead fish on board do not make me feel philosophical. I don't dwell on what their sacrificed lives signify, or try to imagine what it's like to be a fish. As usual, I think of my expenses, and paying off the boat. Also, every six minutes, like the average 22-year-old male human, I think of nooky.

About 7 p.m. I pull up at the buying-station dock. I don't need to toot my whistle. When they see me tying up at the unloading winch, a crew comes down. (They stay late here. Much later than 7 p.m.)

"How'd it go?" one of them asks.

"Didn't go too well," I tell him. "Only got a couple of thousand pounds, mostly coho."

"Yeah, that's what everyone's been getting."

That ends the formalities. I climb down into the fish-hold, where the ice has become a bit slimy and wetter than a week ago. After a couple of minutes, the crew lowers a "bucket" through the hatch. It comes down on the end of a steel cable, like some mechanical spider, with grinding and squeaking noises from the winch.

It's called a bucket, but it's a heavy, rectangular steel box about the size of a washing machine and it can hold 400 pounds of fish.

My job is to pack fish into this spacious receptacle. I dig each salmon out of the ice. I do this carefully, one at a time, and lay each one in the bucket. I might have been tucking children into bed, I was so careful. I don't throw the fish in. I don't want to knock off scales or spoil their look of attractive eatableness.

Each time I fill the bucket, I bellow, "Take it away!"

It takes me an hour and a half to get all the fish out of the hold. I'm not feeling cold, even though it's 30 degrees Fahrenheit in the place. I'm woolled-up, padded as a sheep, with my fuzzy red hat pulled right down. With all that work and moving around, I feel as warm as a boy after a hectic snowball fight.

But I'm not finished yet, no! I have to clean the fish-hold. The fish are gone, but the original three tons of sparkling ice has become three tons of moist and slimy ice. The only way to remove it is to shovel it into the bucket. The crew keeps lowering the bucket, while I toil below like a woolly troll. An hour and a half later, I've shovelled out the ice. I'm crouched in my short rubber boots, in about two inches of freezing water, and pull a plug in the bottom. The slimy liquid drains into a sump in the bilge. (Later

I'll run the bilge pump and contribute the slimy water to the ocean. Some organism is bound to eat it.)

But I'm not finished yet! I need to *clean* the hold. At my command, the crew lowers a fresh-water hose and I give the whole place a dousing. Then I scrub the slimy areas with a stiff brush. I do this with the energetic bustle of a hard-working nurse. For a final dab of quality control, I splash around some bleach. Then hose it away. The idea is to get these white fibreglass walls glittery clean. No germs! Germs that live in fish slime might give the next load of fish a bad smell.

But I'm not finished yet! I need fresh ice. I pull myself out of the hold, stretch and may even groan quietly (it is now about 10 p.m.). I untie the boat and run it down the dock to a chute loader. The crew manoeuvres the chute over the opening to my fish-hold. Ice pours in. Swoosh, rumble, glitter.

One thing remains. Getting *paid*. It's a short walk to the little office building. The windows pour yellow light into the dockyard blackness, like promising beams of gold. Inside, two guys are waiting with my docket. It states the weight of the fish and the price they're paying (this is always fair, because there are many independent and competing buyers). I can ask for cash, or a cheque, or a combination. I take part in cash, because I'll need it for food and fuel tomorrow.

Back to the boat. I run it to one of the free public docks, provided by the government for fishermen. (Ding! One merit point for the Department.)

Exhausted, but fulfilled by payment in full, the noble fisherman falls into bed and is asleep in a minute, right? Not at all. The noble fisherman heads to the pub for a couple of beers.

The next day, I go into the little town, wash my clothes, have a shower, and buy food. Then I fill up with diesel fuel and fresh water. And set off again for the fishing banks.

Repeat the above 26 times. Then stop for the winter.

The off-season

The salmon season closed in September (this was the mid 1960s). How did this 22-year-old fisherman (with his honest features now more weathered) spend his first off-season winter? Living on my boat, in Vancouver Harbour. Certain docks were like a government-sponsored caravan park for fishing boats. I was assigned a slip and assessed a small rent. There were power outlets for electricity, and fresh water from taps. Looxury.

I had earned $9,200, but I still felt pinched. I'd paid off part of the mortgage on my boat. And there were six months of living expenses ahead, expenses for maintaining and "upgrading" the boat, berthing expenses in the harbour, and no income until the next season.

What do I mean by "upgrading" the boat? Remember the Curse of the Auditor? Fuel leaked into the bilge, for example. I'd been cruising up and down the fishing banks, trying to look as happy as I could, trying to ignore the smell of diesel fumes from the bilge. Could anything ignite it down there? Surely not, I believed or trusted. But in that first off-season, I set about finding the leak. This required weeks, with fishermen on the docks lending advice, a helping hand, tools.

There were many other things haywire about that boat. The electrical system was hard to understand, as if it had been done by an enthusiastic but ignorant fisherman instead of an experienced electrician. How could this happen? Ditto for many mechanical devices. Things worked, but many things only just worked.

I built up a resolve to improve all that. Like most fishermen, I couldn't afford tradesmen, so I bought parts, got advice on the docks, and did it all myself. With great enthusiasm. (See? The cycle of unprofessional boat repairs keeps recurring, like a nautical law.) In any case, it was the way folks did things in my boyhood fishing village. They fixed everything themselves. They had almost zero income.

Little by little, I did fix many of *Joy II*'s faults. Other things became haywire again, but in interesting new ways.

When I'd made enough mechanical or electrical progress for a day, I'd work at improving my fishing knowledge. Lessons were available at the pub. I was scared about blowing it next season, ending up in the wrong spot, going broke. This is profound fisherman terror, very primitive and real. Everyone huddled together, swapping stories and hopes. We behaved like a nervous school of fish. If enough fishermen believed anything, it was quickly *true*. Such-and-such bait won't work for such-and-such a fish! But no one might have tried it. A year later, everyone *knew* that bait did work, and was the best bait. Electrical fishing "boosters" were a comic case. (More on that later.)

In the next off-season, I could afford to rent a little apartment. The year after that, I put a deposit on an apartment and started paying it off. This conventional setup made a better impression on the young women I dated than coaxing them to my cramped boat — at the smelly docks, where drunks whistled at them and their high heels might get caught in dock planks.

I lived in Vancouver for six years. In the last two years, I could afford airline tickets and travel outside Canada. I spent time in San Francisco and was a student at San Francisco State College (in Liberal Arts). It was the sixties and I was a student, with money too. Hey ho.

So the years swam by, the salmon ran in their everlasting abundance and I caught my share. If someone who resembled an Old Testament prophet had crawled out of the forest and told me why the salmon season would be cut to three weeks (instead of six months), and would finally go to *zero*, I would have regarded this prophet as needing a cure instead of a refutation. But no such prophet, or anyone else, suggested that. No one smelled any whiff of doom.

At a personal level, instead of Nemesis, I received the opposite: my dad offered his boat to my brother Henry and me. Dad had finished fishing. He was retiring. We could *have* his boat. Right away, Henry told me *I* could have it, because he already had a boat. So I said: great! A 45-foot boat. I could expand operations, have a crew.

So I sold *Joy II* and went back to the village. There was some work to do on my dad's boat. Before saying what happened with that boat, I have to tell you more about commercial fishing. There's no way to understand what went wrong with Canada's fishing industry without peering into all the corners. There is no simple explanation.

2

Modern ways to catch fish

An up-to-date fishing boat carries everything but a Death Ray. The boat is a combination of an advanced military machine and a cold-storage container. The military technology is not sporting, but it's essential. Whoa . . . *essential?* I do not exaggerate. If a boat-owner misses one new trick, falls a little behind, he'll soon be limping financially, then crippled, then probably ruined.

This chapter graphs a curve of fishing-industry madness. The madness rises steeply. And here's the question to brood on, as you observe the inmates start to dance weirdly, gibber, and froth: What brought on this mania?

Electronics

The original electronics on the *Joy II* were lowbrow: one depth-sounding sonar and a single radiophone, to talk to nearby boats. If I had been time-warped from *Joy II* into one of today's boats, I would have felt like a Roman soldier dropped into the Gulf War. What *is* all this stuff?

GPS

The Global Positioning System (GPS) pinpoints the boat's location. It works out the latitude and longitude by listening to incoming satellite signals. It's now accurate to a few feet (people have opinionated views on the exact figure). The device makes a magnetic compass look as old-fashioned as Magellan's hat. But a GPS isn't mainly to stop boats from getting lost at sea. Boats rarely did get lost. What pre-GPS boats *couldn't* do was to find their way back to some exact watery location with 100-percent certainty where fish had been found on an earlier trip.

Take this example. A line of hooks — sometimes miles long — is laid across the sea bottom. The ends are marked with buoys. Then the boat travels off to a new spot — maybe over the horizon — and lays down another line. Which raises the nail-biting question: How can all those buoys be found again? This used to spook me, badly. Before GPS, I'd have to anchor each buoy in a place where I could see at least one other buoy from some other line. I'd end up with 50 or 60 buoys, making a visually-connected network. (Like signal fires, connecting a series of hills.) That meant if I could find *any* buoy again, I could find them all. Because this network sprawled over a considerable seascape, there was a sporting chance I could find my way back to some part of it. Buoy ahoy!

But that was a hassle and it didn't make fishing sense to lay the lines out that way. I might not be laying them where the fish were biting well, but mainly as markers. Another thing: when I was bringing the lines back in, I'd have to stop work earlier than I wanted to. I'd have to find a buoy before it got dark, bring that line in, then stop, because I couldn't usually see a buoy that marked another line. It was out somewhere in the liquid blackness.

When I got a GPS in 1984, I felt so pleased I nearly clutched it to my heart. I could now set each fishing line independently, right where I wanted it. The buoys *didn't* have to be in sight of each other. After I'd anchored each buoy, I'd stride confidently into the cabin and stand in front of my GPS screen. It showed a glowing map of the area, and I'd click to make a new buoy image on the map, exactly where the boat was. When I moved the boat, I left behind real buoys in the water and dot-like buoys on the video map. To find my way back to a buoy, I'd head for it using the screen. And I could do it at night! I'd get the boat close to where the buoy showed on the screen, slow down like I was docking a spacecraft, ease in close, put the engine into neutral, run the searchlight around in the blackness — and there it was, the buoy out there in the water.

There are classy GPSs that can remember routes the boat has travelled. They can even take over and steer the boat to a destination. When I experimented with the steering feature, it was more nuisance to put in the data than to simply use the old autopilot (which worked from the magnetic compass and got fairly close). The autopilot was fine for long trips. For hyper-precision, the equivalent of landing a probe on the asteroid Eros, I'd travel the last few miles using the GPS screen.

It is also said to be possible to use a GPS for creating a log-book. My own GPS manual said so. Every time fish are brought in, just enter those facts in the computer, press this and that, and lo — an automatic logbook entry! The exact location, time, number of fish. Except it refused to do that. I tried on three different days, allowing for it to get used to my personality. But it never worked. I'd sit there with a sullen expression, glaring at the manual, with my old red hat on for comfort.

"What if the GPS breaks down?" Some people ask this, with certain twitches and signs of worry. Relax. It just means the skipper won't know *exactly* where his boat is. He still knows *pretty* well, because there's the magnetic compass and also a radio system called LORAN. Anyway, most boats have two GPSs, sometimes three. They aren't expensive. Boats carry a spare GPS the same way they carry a spare fan belt.

LORAN

LORAN enchanted me when it was finally available for *Joy II*.

I'd been running the boat for four years using the magnetic compass. My new LORAN unit — fundamentally a smart radio receiver — worked out the boat's position by comparing radio beams from different land stations. (LORAN wasn't invented by Lorraine. It means LOng-RAnge Navigation system.) It showed latitude and longitude, in glowing numbers, in a little display window. It seemed magic.

LORAN didn't work well close to shore (within ten miles, it started to falter). And it didn't work at night because the ionosphere blurs, so the radio beams get bounced wrong and arrive punch-drunk. Also, the system never worked *way* out at sea — at about 600 miles, that was the end of LORAN. Mind you, those range limitations didn't disturb me in *Joy II* (600 miles out! — I rarely got 60 miles out). But I felt keenly deprived in my next boat when I chased tuna 1,000 miles out and LORAN just hissed white noise.

The accuracy of LORAN was to about a quarter of a mile. That's in places where the reception was good, and only in daytime. So I could find a buoy in daylight: LORAN got me within a quarter of a mile, then I could see the buoy.

Video-screen fishfinders

Ahab would have been profoundly stirred if he'd seen a fishfinder. What a way to find a deceitful, evasive whale! Fishfinders send out sonar beams at different frequencies, listen for the echoes, calculate in a constant frenzy, and display their discoveries on a colour screen. A large school of fish (or a whale) is a fuzzy red blob against the sky-blue background of the screen. Different sorts of fish can sometimes be discriminated. A school of sockeye salmon, for example, showed on my screen as the Greek letter lambda (or upside-down V). Single fish could often be seen — a darker blue spot against the light-blue background, and of course the fish moved. One sort of fish that *didn't* show up, or just fleetingly, was tuna. They moved too fast. The tuna came and went, almost between electronic blinks.

Peering into my fishfinder screen, filled with high spirits, I could admire the passing sea bottom, like a Caribbean tourist in a glass-bottom boat. I could note the large rocks and sudden underwater cliffs. I could see fishing gear I was trailing — the weights and lures. Schools of fish — red smears — streaked up and down, stopped to check out the lures, then stayed to nibble and bite, or changed their minds and took off. I fished as if I had supernatural powers. I could run my lines within a few feet of the bottom, tempting the fish there. I pulled my gear through underwater canyons, letting the lures pass close to rock faces, where fish lurked in caves. Come . . . greedily devour the treacherous bait.

Fishfinders can be programmed to buzz or beep when a large school of fish moves. The annoying part is the false alarms, like having a too-touchy burglar alarm. I'd carefully program the alarm, finally get its sensitive nerves adjusted just right, then the weather would roughen and the boat would start bouncing. Bubbles under the boat totally confused the system. Master, there's a gigantic school right under the hull! Beep, beep, beepedy-beep!

A fishfinder would have helped me some on *Joy II*, if such devices had been available. But not as much as it would have helped competing boats that had a crew. Anyway, these days the skipper of a big boat concentrates on the screen, steers with Ahab-like intensity, pursues blue dots and red swarms and Greek lambdas while the crew outside hauls in surprised fish.

Radar

Now let's rise above the water line.

Radar was another electronic instrument *not* found on *Joy II*. When I got a radar (on my next boat), I was beguiled. I could even follow single seagulls! Obviously that wasn't its most important use. The point was to keep from ramming boats in fog, or at night. I could also navigate close to shore. With the radar and fishfinder *both on*, I could run the boat in a black and foggy night through a twisting lagoon.

Historical comparison: in *Joy II*, my bravest navigation by instruments was to use the depth sounder and follow a conspicuous underwater ridge (the 30-fathom ridge). It ran for 40 miles, right along the coast. If I followed that, I'd be safe from rocks and shallows (but still risked ramming other boats).

Radio communications

Yes, the marine radio-communication systems are now fabulous! Yes, fisherman use them a lot! It's *how* they use them that's extraordinary or dismaying.

For long distances, fishermen use what's called "single sideband" radio. It reaches several thousand miles. For shorter range, they use another sort —VHF. We also had CBs and every species of private cell phone. We wanted every radio communication system we could buy! I had *ten* different sorts of radiophones on my last boat — in order to *lie*! And listen in!

Competing fishing boats are like nations on the brink of war. They keep talking, but don't give anything away. The intention of communication is to confound and confuse. Everyone also *listens* hard, hoping someone will goof and let useful tips slip out.

This was a vast elaboration of the obfuscating CB exchanges I told you about on *Joy II* in that example between me and Charlie. The obfuscation grew, then darkened and wrapped itself in innumerable folds and complexities with each upgrade in communication technology. We were almost rendered speechless by the implications of overwhelming technical capacity. By the time I was fishing in my second boat, 29 of my mates on other boats plus myself (the "Gang of 30") formed a private group to share information. *Keeping* the information private was the problem. First we communicated using CB radio, on a channel that seemed forgotten and obscure. That only worked for four days. They found us. We next concocted simple codes that could be blended into a normal conversation. "I'm fed up with fried eggs" might mean "Sockeye are biting like mad!" But the snoopers figured it out. And it didn't take them long. If fishermen aren't catching anything, they're like bored and hungry prisoners — time weighs on them, they have unused ingenuity that's looking for outlets, and a great motivation to escape from their sorry situation.

The Gang of 30 next tried a WW II enigma-machine approach: we each built an identical code wheel. It could generate thousands of codes for every phrase we might want to use. With everyone's wheel set to the same position, we could read off the same code for "Coho aren't biting here at all." That might be "RL37." The next day we'd reset our code wheels to another position, according to a system we'd worked out and written down. (It was inspired by the way code books were used in nuclear subs, that we'd read about in the Sunday papers.) So the new "coho aren't biting" code might be "BJ91." That would confound the snoopers, right?

It sure did. It also confused the Gang of 30. We continually messed up and got our code wheels set wrong. Not a day passed that some guys didn't rush off to fish where there weren't any, or inform everyone they weren't catching anything when they were doing great.

We gave up on that one. Instead, we all bought scrambler phones. We got them from England, and they came with a guarantee that the scrambling system couldn't be broken. It was the same variety of scrambler used by the British armed forces, we were advised. True, we never had evidence that our conversations were intercepted and decoded. But decoding our *own* conversations was sometimes hard. I'd have my ear to the phone as it unscrambled an incoming secret message. It might sound like "Here's a sssssssss ing but ffffffffffsss later than pfffffffffffsss, OK?" There were always five or six guys who couldn't make out what had been said.

So there'd be information leakage, because we had to broadcast on an open channel in order to clear up confusions. Or one of us would talk to a buddy not in the group, and use an open channel. Other private groups and fishing clans all had the same problems and they all carried on like this too. That's why I had ten radiophones! I'd madly switch from one to another, listening to different channels, trying to pick up someone who was careless. A stray word or revealing phrase. Any hint. I sometimes got an earful.

TV ... not

Satellite TV couldn't be made to work right, because of the incessant heaving of the boat. Instead we had a VCR in the galley. At night, we'd usually watch videos (King Kong III, Revenge of the Squid From Hell . . .). Most boat crews did the same.

Weather monitor

Maybe a gift for the skipper who has everything? A weather monitor digitally displays bad or good news about the weather, without the skipper having to go outside and hold up a wet finger. It shows things like wind speed and direction, and wind chill. I never owned one of these novelties. Pointless, I thought — just look out the window. Or listen to the weather forecasts on the radio, if you don't believe what you see.

This all means ...

With all these sensors, rotating radar eyes and super-sharp

sonar ears, and the GPS doing everything but writing the boat's location in day-glo numbers in the water, fishermen grew outrageously efficient. Anyone could do it. The masterly old-time fishermen of my long-gone boyhood weren't unique anymore. After two years on a boat, any alert 20-year-old could catch fish as well as the old-timers. This point matters. And because this isn't a detective story, I don't need to hide the clues: *This hyper-efficiency is one hint about why certain fish stocks have almost disappeared.* But don't jump to conclusions — more clues to come! This is an involved mystery we have here.

Trollers

"Trolling" was what I did in *Joy II:* cruising through the water, dragging behind me lines of hooks and lures. (From the antique French word "troller" — to run about.)

The big modern trollers usually have more lines than I had on *Joy II*. And a big boat can stay out longer, if they freeze the fish solid instead of packing them in ice. So the boat can travel further — hundreds of miles out, instead of the 50 or 60 miles I used to venture in *Joy II*.

When I moved up to bigger boats and had a crew, I'd steer hundreds of miles out and look for tuna. We trolled with a few lures right behind the boat and we flew along. Speed attracts the swift tuna. To haul them in (they weigh about 25 pounds each), we used a little hydraulic puller. We *always* froze them, because of the long time we were out there. These big fish aren't gutted and cleaned: their digestive system doesn't harm the meat, so they're frozen just as they are ("in the round").

Closer to the coast, we'd troll for salmon. But with our big boat we'd clean hundreds of fish a day, instead of the 50 or so I used to catch in *Joy II*. This meant there were impressive clouds of seagulls. We got to know some of these entertaining spirits of the air. One bird might have only a single leg, and have trouble managing a fast, duck-like landing in the water because of its unbalanced leg-drag. There were birds with peculiar beaks or uncommon colours — nature trying out mutations to see what happened. None of the birds, whether standard or odd, landed on the boat for long. It made them seasick. (A free fact for the scientists at the Department of Fisheries and Oceans.)

We'd catch and freeze about 40,000 pounds of salmon (instead of *Joy II*'s 2,500 pounds). And all that would be frozen hard, not just chilled in crushed ice. The hold stayed at -30 degrees Fahrenheit (ten degrees lower and we would have frozen the mercury in our thermometers). We froze the catch so hard because we'd all learned the secret: freeze them fast and keep them at polar temperatures, and you get top quality.

I'm talking about trollers in general — big ones — so I'd better reveal their biggest general hassle: keeping the freezer working.

Troller

The freezers caused non-stop anxiety. The first freezers used in fishing boats were exactly the same ones used in refrigerated trucks. The boat owner would just buy a truck freezer and whang it in (and whang and whang). They were hard to fit into a boat, usually too small to do the job anyway, and sickeningly unreliable. This fact amazed every skipper, as he scratched his salty forehead, because the freezers worked *fine* on trucks. After those failures, other (cheap) freezer systems were tried. All were born unto trouble. About 65 percent of our time on the radio was spent moaning about our freezers, offering advice, asking for sympathy, sighing and almost breaking down in fits of rare male sensitivity. In time, we became adept freezer-fixers. We'd set out with expert tools and cylinders of Freon.

Typical offshore scene: a quarter-inch copper cooling tube breaks, and Freon roars out — a stupendous geyser. There's $2,000 dollars worth of Freon in the system, so I lurch around the engine room like a monkey with rabies, shutting things off, trying to find the right valve. And finally do.

Boats were always losing fishing time because of faulty freezers. Freezers had many ways of dying. New freezer diseases seemed to appear every week, unknown to medical freezer science. Baffled, the boat owner would have to hustle to shore, unload the fish, and then get the damn thing fixed. There was one ray of grace in all this: a frozen load would last a couple of days, even with a dead freezer. The boat's insulation was Everest-rated.

It could be said that we inflicted this freezer hell on ourselves — we bought such cheap freezers! But most of us had no choice. Boats our size couldn't afford a Freezer of Distinction that cost hundreds of thousands of dollars. Indeed, there are classy freezers on the enormous fleet boats and those freezers presumably work just fine. (*Enormous fleet boats?* . . . Patience. They come later — additional agents of Nemesis.)

The salmon we caught were still cleaned and packed with the same care I used in *Joy II*. But, as I said, frozen hard instead of packed with ice. The fish still had to look good — for one thing, they often ended up in sushi bars in Japan. No missing scales, no blood on them, no sea lice hanging off them.

Long-liners

I've mentioned long-lining: lines of hooks — miles long — left on the sea bottom, marked with buoys at both ends.

That's the only way to catch halibut. Because it's the only way that's *allowed*. Halibut fishing is controlled by a joint American and Canadian commission (dating from the 1880s). Long-lining works fine, because halibut hang around on the sea bottom. But in the 1950s a competing and more deadly method appeared (dragging, which I'll get to in a minute). The commission pondered and eventually outlawed anything but long-lining. Their stand was a godsend. The halibut are still there, in a big way.

Bringing in the halibut from these long lines of hooks resembles harvesting work done by Czarist peasants. (Halibut fishermen say that the ideal physique for a great halibut fisherman is a strong body, but no head.) The mark of professionalism in long-lining is *not* to stop the gurdy once it starts to reel in the line. One husky fisherman watches the line coming in and unsnaps each hook, empty or not. If there's a fish on it, he gaffs it and then unsnaps the hook. There's another halibut expert standing right behind him. He grabs the jerking fish with his hairy hand, kills and guts it. Another expert takes it into the hold and packs it in ice. (The ice-packing method was like I used in *Joy II* — but with more ice, more fish, and a lot more work.) We never froze halibut. They kept well in ice and the market wanted fresh ones. We'd stay out 10 or 12 days and the fish were still in top condition.

Long-lining works with any bottom-dwelling fish. To zero in

on a single type of fish, it's a matter of choosing the bait and the right size of hook. For halibut, we used octopus as bait (halibut love it, but other fish love it less). And we used large hooks. Halibut are big, and the large hooks made it harder for smaller fish to get caught. When all this is done right, the "by-catch" (the fish you *don't* want) amounts to one percent or so. And when we found a rich halibut ground, there'd rarely be anything but halibut on the hooks: because the halibut had already *eaten* all the smaller fish.

Another point: after a halibut gets hooked, it can be down there for a long time. Half a day, even a whole day. So their fight had usually flickered out by the time we got them to the surface. Nevertheless, they were alive. That is, unless we were unlucky (and the halibut were unlucky) and we happened to be fishing where the sea lice prowled. These fiends are about an inch long. They look like slugs when they crawl out of their little shells. The shells crack agreeably if you step on them, which I used to do merrily. (I need to explain that the sea lice I mentioned earlier, the ones that attach to salmon, are much smaller and don't harm the salmon much — just nibble their scales a bit.) But if a hooked halibut is found by a gang of the fiendish sea lice, the halibut is eaten alive. Except for the skin, which the lice don't like. When we took such a "halibut" off the hook, it was a bag of skin with hundreds of wriggling sea lice inside.

But that's not the only thing that could go wrong. The lines could snag on the seabed. With miles of hooks lying on the seabed, you'd expect that to happen. It did. We'd run the boat in a circle, keeping the snagged line tight, trying to unhook it and edge it out. If it broke, we got part of it back. Then we'd go to the other marker buoy and bring up that section of line, or as much as we could. We ended up with heavily spliced lines, with new sections inserted from our stock of fishing line.

To avoid those snags and horrors, the solution is to pick a perfect halibut ground. They can be found anywhere from close to shore to about 40 miles out. We'd look for a sea-bottom that wouldn't snag the hooks, like gravel. (Fortunately halibut like gravel.) And a place with no sea lice.

Halibut are consistent. When we found a good spot, the halibut would be there every year at definite times.

Seiners

Picture this: a circle in the water, 500 feet across, with a net hanging down from it 200 feet into the water. The net hangs down like a gigantic tin can with both ends cut out, held up by plastic floats about the size of seagulls. There's a rope that runs along the net at the surface, following the floats, and a second rope along the bottom of the net. The bottom one passes through brass rings attached to the net. It's nylon because nylon sinks, and slides through the rings easily.

That arrangement is called a "seine net." A seine boat (a "seiner") sets this up by running in a circle, playing out net. Sometimes the colour of the floats changes at regular distances along the circle — making a colour-coded guide for the skipper as he looks back, steers, and judges his circle (a jaunty sight when it's all done, with the different colours of floats bobbing in their wide circle).

Winching in the lower line draws the bottom of the net together. This traps any fish swimming in

Seiner

there. The net now has the concave shape of a noodle strainer. Then the top line is winched in from one end, so the circle of floats gets smaller and smaller. The net finally shrinks to a large bag of fish in the water, right by the boat. The bag is dragged up a ramp at the stern by using a "drum" (a big winch), or lifted right up into the air using a boom that swings over the deck. The bag may have 10,000 fish in it — six or seven tons. The net is synthetic, tough, and takes all this easily.

The fish are then spilled onto the deck. There's not much variety among them. That may sound odd, because the fishing method seems indiscriminate: anything inside the net gets caught. But there are several reasons why the catch tends to be uniform. First, there are no bottom fish, because the net doesn't hang down that far (it's never used where it might touch bottom). Second, it's always a net *designed* to catch one sort of fish. For example, there are standard nets for salmon and herring. (Any of these nets are expensive — maybe $80,000 each — so a boat doesn't carry a wide variety, or spares.) Another fundamental reason for the lack of variety in the catch: the net tends to trap a whole school of fish, or part of one. Schools don't mix, and rarely swim close to each other. And salmon often swim in orderly corridors of their own choosing, like underwater rivers. So the net intercepts part of a corridor. Herring school tightly, because each herring tries to get into the centre of the school for protection. When a seiner catches herring, it's close to 100 percent herring, plus a couple of predators from outside the school.

The few misfits in the catch are thrown overboard. But the fish that are kept, the bulk of them, aren't usually in great shape — most have scales knocked off. But in any disaster, some individuals come through OK, like those grains of wheat that emerge untouched from between millstones. A few of the fish look perfect. They're usually kept separate and sold into the lucrative fresh-fish market. The rest go into a hold that's filled with freezing water. They *aren't* gutted and cleaned. No time — this is hectic "madhouse" fishing, where the Department allows only a few hours of fishing at a time. It's a system that yields reasonable sizes of catches, fishermen with nervous tics and conditions, and poor-quality fish. Everything in the hold goes to a cannery.

The Department of Fisheries and Oceans limits the length of net as well as dictates the days and hours it can be used — maybe just eight hours every second week, during a certain season. If a boat didn't use the maximum allowed net length, it wouldn't be competitive. But to handle a net of maximum size, the boat needs to have a big drum to winch it in, big motors and husky hydraulics. Not to mention having enough boat-bulk so it doesn't tip over when it lifts the net carrying all those dripping tons. Seiners are 50 to 90 feet long (compared to *Joy II*'s 32 feet).

Gillnetters

The gillnet (or "drift net") hangs in the water like a suspended volleyball net. Fish of the right size put their heads through the holes in the net and get caught by their gills. Simple! Its only use in Canada is to catch salmon. In Canadian waters it's typically 1,800 feet long, but not very deep (by regulation). The top is held up with white plastic floats (so they can be seen easily) and the bottom is held down with lead weights. It's attached to the boat and trails behind, because regulations forbid anchoring a gillnet and leaving it. At the far end is a buoy, with a light on it — gillnetting is usually done at night. In daylight, most fish would see the net and wouldn't get caught. Fish can sometimes see it by bright moonlight too, and the catch can be poor.

The crew has to keep an eye on the net, because it can stray into artistic but useless hairpin bends and curvy swirls. That shortens the net's fish-catching area. Also, other boats could run into the net; they have to be warned away. Red are the eyeballs that look after a gillnet boat.

At dawn, the net is wound in from a drum on the stern. The crew grab each fish and pull it out by hand. I haven't done gillnetting, but I'm told that the fish and crew can be equally grumpy at this stage. The fish definitely aren't in good shape after a night in the net. They've lost both spirit and scales, so they're fated for the cannery, not the fresh-fish market.

Gillnetter (From the collection of the Vancouver Maritime Museum)

There is a type of gillnet that the fish *can't* see, even in daylight: monofilm. But it's banned in Canada, and offshore by international agreement. (Some cheaters are still caught in the vast Pacific and fined large sums.) The Japanese and Taiwanese once used monofilms on a formidable scale in the mid-Pacific, each boat running miles of nets. They sometimes claimed they were fishing for squid, but mainly seemed to be after salmon. There were more than 1,000 boats north of Hawaii. Trouble came when it was found they were catching thousands of birds that dove underwater to catch the trapped fish. Not to mention dolphins, which got themselves wrapped up in the net. So gillnet fishing in international waters was banned in 1991 by the UN General Assembly. Most countries soon set their own rules for gillnets in their territorial waters, if they hadn't already done that.

Draggers

This is the brute-force end of fishing. A boat with stupendous horsepower drags along an immense net that's open at the front like a scoop. The net might be dragged along the sea bottom, or at any higher level. Sometimes 20,000 pounds of fish at a time are caught (yes, 10 tons; it's a heap). Compare that with maybe *two* tons for a whole *week's* fishing on *Joy II*.

Dragger/Trawler (From the collection of the Vancouver Maritime Museum)

Now picture "Curly," the skipper — and owner — of a dragger. He's 25 and he's paying off a mortgage on this 1,000-horsepower boat. Propelled by 1,000 horsepower and chased by his terrifying mortgage, nothing stops Curly. Not even a coral bed, for example. I assure you that it's hard to fish in a coral bed, because the fish can hide — and lines or nets get snagged. But Curly has a solution: instead of dragging a net (which might tear, even if it's made of super-tough Kevlar), he first drags a steel cable across the coral. An "otter board" on each end of this cable acts like a tiller, pulling the ends of the cable in opposite directions and keeping the cable tight. The heavy cable slices the coral like a wire cheese-cutter that's 300 feet across. Gigantic forces develop in the coral and bits fly everywhere. Curly serenely turns the boat and connects his superior Kevlar drag net. Then he hurtles back toward the smashed coral. The drag net puffs up underwater into a giant mouth that runs along the sea bottom, 300 feet across and 200 feet high. The fish that used to live in the coral are swimming in confused loops, looking for home. The net scoops them up.

This comprehensive strategy can only be applied once per coral bed. While it's possible to debate whether or not coral beds are a good thing to have in the ocean, there's something else in the ocean that Curly, um . . . changes permanently. It's the sea-bottom itself. When a drag net crosses the bottom, it ploughs the area. Whether the bottom is gravel, mud or sand, the results are unhealthy. The organic balance is upset. A fertile fish-feeding expanse turns into a "sour bottom" — an underwater desert. But this is denied in a blustery but whining tone by most draggers. "We're just plowing, like farmers do. It's good for the sea bottom!" Meanwhile, troubled souls at the Department of Fisheries and Oceans stare and say: "We haven't done any studies. We don't know anything about it." (Studies done in Europe and the Caribbean on the effects of dragging don't seem to count.)

Fishermen who *aren't* draggers might not grumble, if their own fishing wasn't being hurt. But they do grumble, because they notice a thing or two. I can tell you what the fishing was like in some places 40 years ago. How reliable it was, year after year. And how it died after draggers had ploughed the place for enough years. It takes about ten years to make a thoroughly sour bottom. But no one keeps records of these slow-moving changes. It only lives in the heads of a few old-timers.

Here's one sorry case: the "Goose Island Bank." It's an underwater gravel bank and it used to swarm with halibut. When F. Heward Bell, head of the Halibut Commission, retired in 1970, he wrote a book: *The Pacific Halibut — The Resource and Fishery.* He points out that the Goose Island Bank yielded about 500 million pounds of halibut since it was first fished in 1903. In the 1970s, the catches dropped to less than 1 million pounds a year, from over 7 million before that. I saw this process myself.

In the 1960s, Canada only had a three-mile limit and there was an invasion of Japanese and Russian draggers (which are also known as "trawlers"). They were hard at it for about a decade, until the Canadian fishing limit was pushed out to 200 miles (an international result of the Cod War between Iceland and Britain). During the 1970s, Canadian draggers started working on the bank too. I tried long-lining there in the 1980s, but couldn't find a single halibut! It was a dead mudbank. By then the draggers had moved to the deeper Goose Island "Gully," west of the bank, where there were still fish.

I demanded an explanation from a manager at the Department of Fisheries and Oceans, my large shadow falling on his desk. He told me: "Oh, lots of halibut still come from Goose Island!"

"Where?" I asked.

"The Goose Island Gully."

I said: "I meant the Goose Island *Bank*! What happened there?"

He said, "I didn't know anyone ever fished there."

It had been destroyed before he got his job. Five hundred million pounds of fish had come out of the Goose Island Bank, and he didn't know "anyone ever fished there."

I can picture what forestry would be like if it were handled like dragging. Here's the procedure: first find a native forest, an old one. Then smash it with some gargantuan machine that crunches down trees in footprints the size of a football field, and also chews up the ground. Scoop up all the trees, broken logs, branches, splinters, and pick out a few specimens that seem worth gathering.

After one "harvest" like that, they'd all be in jail!

Draggers winch their whole scoopful of fish up a ramp at the stern. They dump all those tons onto the deck and do a rough sort to see what they've got. If they find anything dangerous, like a live shark, they delete its life — then throw the reject overboard. A lot of the catch is already dead: in the great scoop, there may have been 100 tons of panicked fish, jammed together. They may have been dragged along for eight hours before the scoop was pulled up. Then whizzed up from 3,000 feet. An eye-popping jolt, even for a fish.

So here are the dragger crew, still walking around through this life-challenged catch, picking out the ones to toss overboard. They jab those with a "pew" — a handle with steel spike sticking out the end, like the implement that park attendants use to pick up waste paper. The remaining OK fish are then heaved into a hold of freezing water. Most of them end up in filleting plants, where they'll be turned into fish sticks and other delicacies. There are also fish processors that specialize in very bony and mushy fish (if you can picture that combination). They make the fish into artificial crab. The fish are ground up, then washed and rewashed until all the flavour and colour is gone. A tasteless mush. They add stabilizer, colouring and flavour. Crab meat!

So what's the good news about dragging? It isn't *allowed* for some kinds of fish, or in some places. And the draggers themselves aren't menacing characters in black balaclavas. They're usually fun to talk to, normal, often generous. ("Another beer for everybody!") Mark, Fred, Harry, Luke, and Curly. They might have been crewing on a long-lining boat before they got into dragging. Or they owned their own troller — and began to smolder with heretical questions about the amount of time it takes to catch one fish at a time on a hook.

All sorts of guys have jumped into dragging. It looks more profitable (and is). It takes less fishing skill. Sometimes the big fishing companies pay for the boats, in exchange for part of the catch — as if the fishermen had become tenant farmers or possibly serfs. Also, the Department of Fisheries and Oceans encouraged dragging when it was starting in the 1960s and 1970s. They paid subsidies up to 50 percent to build the boats. This generosity was prompted by reports from government scientists who went googly-eyed about the tons of fish "out there" that draggers would be able to catch, and that weren't being caught by old-fashioned methods.

With these stimulants and temptations, who'd blame Mark, Fred, Harry, Luke, and Curly for their occupational choice? They weren't doing anything illegal. On the contrary, their pursuit was encouraged. They saw an opportunity, they often put up their own money or got a mortgage on their house, they took a business risk, and they were in it as a business. The opportunity beckoned. The takings could be huge. They had every encouragement except an advertising leaflet from King Neptune.

All those facts can be assembled into another clue about what went wrong with Canada's fishing industry. Here are these normal people, looking after their ordinary interests, but working within a system that's malformed so that it brings warped and unintended results. It has to be said that the same vindication (or excuse) applies to the folks who work at the Department of Fisheries and Oceans. They are mainly conscientious and some are luminously bright, but the rules they work by — the system itself— has a history, a karma, a life force of its own. They're obligated to move with it, in some cases to justify what's gone before, or simply to try to make sense of their own intricate paper creation. Also, the managers at the Department change fairly quickly, compared to the time it takes to see a changed trend in fishing stocks. You or me or anyone who was inserted into one of those roles — dragger or bureaucrat — might behave the same way.

As an illustration, with some irresistible ridicule, let's consider the story of the thorn fish. But first I need to note the Department's loyalty to the UN's "Precautionary Principle" in fishing. One Department official explained it to me this way: "It means you won't fish a stock unless you know how much fish is there and the safe level to take from it." Splendid! Makes perfect sense. That's wisdom for you. The UN asked the world to fish that safe way and Canada agreed, putting important signatures at the bottom of the papers.

Meanwhile, in the cold depths lives the thorn fish — a fish that lives so deep it looks like it's been scrunched. I don't wish to offend the Thorn Fish Lovers Society, but this fish is ugly. I'd been making a face and throwing them overboard for 20 years. I rarely caught one, they were oddities, and they all went over the side. Then one day a deck hand informed me, "The buyers are going for these. The Japanese like to eat them!" Our cook was standing there and bravely suggested, "If the Japanese eat them, let's try one." It turned out to be the most delicious fish!

When the draggers found out, which was years later, they went on red alert. They'd been getting hard-up for stock and they de-cided to pursue thorn fish. Yet this presented a challenge. The thorn

fish live about 4,000 feet down, and there was just the occasional
thorn fish to be found in that underwater desert — like rare liz-
ards in the Gobi desert. Undaunted, the draggers towed day and
night, up and down long stretches like they were mowing a vast
lawn. Sure enough, they'd catch a few hundred pounds of thorn
fish a day. Not much weight, but worth it because of the money
they got.

What about the cherished UN principle? To this day, the Department has no idea of the weight of thorn fish down there (the
"biomass" as they gravely and abstractly put it) or the fish's breeding rate, or anything else. Certain rare data does emerge, but not
from the Department. I knew a fisherman who caught a thorn fish
when he was long-lining, and instead of eating it or selling it, he
took it to a laboratory and had its age estimated. He did it from a
mixture of curiosity and fury (about the draggers scooping up so
many of the creatures). The fish was 23 years old! When there are
fish that old in the stock, it's only safe to catch a tiny percentage
of them.

Ah, but I've forgotten something! After much criticism and
rage from environmentalists, the Department came up with what
might be called the General Solution to Drag Net Fishing, Including the Special Case of the Thorn Fish: *Put an observer on each
dragger to see what's caught and how much.* How simple! Soon
every dragger had an Official Person, standing on deck, methodi-
cally and gloomily taking notes. The dragger had to pay for this
service. Here was some outsider with the soul of a customs officer, who might even be a woman — requiring separate toilets
and possibly toned-down deck language.

You may wonder: This is *management?* This is following UN
principles? Sure! . . . sort of. Can't you see the Department is doing something? They are collecting data. True, no idea has been
formed about what ages of fish are being caught, how well they're

breeding, or the b-b-b-b-biomass. The solution is just to let the draggers catch what they caught last year! What could be fairer? It may kill off the stock, or it may not. Then we'll all know, Citizens of Canada.

The note-taking officials on board *do* find that the draggers bring up a lot of by-catch. The crew then throw those back, dead (or nearly). But the Department is satisfied, because they have "someone on the boat." It resolves the issue. Even if it does nothing to reduce the by-catch. Instead, there's a perfect solution: just count the by-catch!

There's also another principle illustrated here: nature works to restore any lunacy that temporarily disappears. The Russians used to have a worldwide fishing fleet and I used to see their boats off Alaska. We had friendly exchanges, sort of. But the Russian's natural fishermanly charm was chilled by a Communist Party member on board: an official observer, with the same status as the skipper. All day, Comrade Spectre haunted the boat and took notes.

The comrade-on-the-boat lunacy has now passed from Russia to Canada.

Gradually I am describing the players in this fish-decline saga, the forces, people's pressing interests and fixations. All these interactions produced forces that crushed and shut down cod fishing in Eastern Canada, killed off the salmon in the areas I used to fish in *Joy II*, not to mention abalone, the cod in the Gulf of Georgia, and a number of "minor" fish.

As you see, the plot is thickening.

Sport fishing

I can tell you there were 267,113 "tidal" sport-fishing licences sold in British Columbia in 1998/99. (There were also 308,393 freshwater licences, but let's concentrate on the tidal ones.)

	Me on *Joy II* in 1964	"Average" tidal sport fisherman (guessing like mad) in 1999
Technical matters		
Fishing days per year	100	10
Fishing hours per day	18	3
Number of lines	6	1
Number of hooks per line	7	1
Fish caught per hour	3	0.0833333
Length of boat	32 feet	20 feet
Power of boat's engine	80 hp	150 hp
Lures used?	Yes, correct for the fish	Yes, correct for the fish
Radar on board?	no	no
GPS on board?	no	yes
Fishfinder on board?	no	yes
Animal spirits		
Dedication to catching as many fish as possible	100%	4%
Accurate knowledge about where to find fish	Extremely good	Fair to hopeless
Is fishing carried out at night?	You bet	No, are you crazy?

Omigod! No wonder those fish stocks are dying! True, that's a lot of sport fishermen, doubtless enthusiastic, and many with skill. But just compare them with a commercial fisherman, even with me on the small boat *Joy II* (see chart on previous page).

Because some places are so popular with sport fishermen, and others are never visited, these fishermen have an uneven effect. Some fishing grounds must be clobbered, others are untouched. For example, lots of sport fishermen stay in waters close to the city of Vancouver. And they mainly go for salmon (certainly not thorn fish!). They also catch halibut and a little cod.

Most sport fishermen think that they can't affect the stock, because they only "catch a few fish." But if 267,113 sport fishermen always had to wear a day-glo fish logo on their forehead, they would become better acquainted with their numbers. And the argument that "I only catch a few" might sound unconvincing to themselves.

We don't know exactly where these folks fish or what they catch (unlike commercial fishermen, whose catch at least is recorded — though the "where it came from" data is obviously not easy to get). What can be said? Well, that mob of tidal sport fishermen *must* be having some effect.

And I need to say one other thing: sport fishing has great political power, and it's pretty unregulated. There are big sports lodges all over the coast. Important citizens are members. The lodges don't have to be licensed, there's not much of a limit on the amount of fish caught.

The story for salmon is revealing. When the salmon numbers started falling, the Department first restricted the trollers and the gillnetters (they're small independent boats, with no political force). Then the seiners. Finally they put some weak regulation on sport fishing of salmon.

3

OK, what *did* happen to the salmon?

> *Salmon stocks are dwindling, and nobody's quite*
> *sure why. This loss can sometimes feel as if there's*
> *a hole in the collective soul.*
> — from *City of Glass*, Douglas Coupland's book about Vancouver

Folks, I know what happened to those fish. But this will take a while. First, here's a clinching statistic: British Columbia took 1 percent of the world's salmon catch in 1999, compared to 15 percent twenty years earlier. *So a few years ago we used to catch 15 times as much of the world's salmon!* Those glum souls in the City of Glass aren't imagining things. Our fish are gone.

Allow me to start with the most "duh . . . " question. Have the salmon sneakily moved, maybe even taken off to some other *country*? (We've heard these fish can swim a long way.)

Well, point one: we aren't dealing with magical beings. We're dealing with a primitive type of fish, with remarkable but rigid instincts. So that's where to start — getting to know how they make their way in the world, if everyone leaves them alone.

Mother Nature's salmon cycle

I've mentioned three sorts of salmon: sockeye, chinook, and coho. They roam the Pacific. Two more sorts roam there too: pink salmon and chum. I used to fish for chum, but pink weren't popular in the fresh-fish market, so I didn't go after those. (Some seiners did and sold big tonnages to canneries.)

Those five sorts had a common ancestor 100 million years ago. Ancestor salmon swam in the same rivers that dinosaurs drank from. The ancestor fish looked strikingly like the sockeye and other salmon in our fresh-fish markets today. Any Vancouver sport fisherman who pulls a sockeye off a hook is holding a fish that still has an antediluvian air bladder and spineless fins from its dinosaur days. (Other fish, like sunfish, have moved on.) The point is that salmon have a long past and deep-set ways. This is important in working out what happened to them in the last 20 years.

All salmon breed in fresh water. That's not likely to surprise you. But this fact may: the mother fish carries approximately one pound of eggs (yeah, whew). She finds her way back to the spot where she was born, picks out a patch of just-so gravel and then carpet-bombs part of her eggs over the area. A male fish keeps an eye on this. He waits for her to move off, then he moves in. He squirts sperm all over the place. Several males may do this, and we can imagine they glare at each other. All this work or fun is repeated up to seven times, for different (but nearby) gravel patches. The active parties then retire to a quiet pool and in a few days, drop dead.

The fertilized eggs in the gravel — seemingly inert, but now profoundly busy — look like cloudy glass beads, tinted orange or red. In five to ten weeks, they hatch. Tiny creatures come out that look fragile, with oversized eyes like bubbles. These unpromising and squirmy things hide in the gravel, while they nibble leftovers from the egg's yoke sac. When they're feeling brave enough, or hungry enough, the small fish pop out of the gravel and start to munch aquatic insects or larvae, or suck plankton (young sockeye do that). Later the young salmon attack other fish — any that are small enough to get down.

Chum are only satisfied with this freshwater life for a few hours or days. (Fish hatcheries in Alaska and Japan take advantage of that. I'll explain later.) Other sorts of salmon stay in fresh water as long as three years — but not usually at their birthplace. They move to a freshwater lake, if they can find one.

For them all, a certain day comes and 100-million-year-old genes light up. The fish head for the sea — or I might say they "tail" for the sea, because the small ones are often swept tail-first down the rivers, as if they want to keep pointing back toward their birthplace. Most of them brave a long trip, sometimes hundreds of miles, with age-old menaces. They get snapped up by large fish, or gulls, herons, otters, and sometimes eels. Man-made perils can be added, but I want to concentrate on what happened before people showed up with their hooks and dams.

In the ocean, they range a long way, or maybe not so far, depending on what sort of salmon they are. Pink salmon rarely get more than 1,500 miles from their home river. They stay in salt water less than a year. Chinook may go 2,500 miles and stay out seven years.

I also need to point out what they eat. All this information is essential. Sockeye, pink and chum are gluttons for plankton, topped off with some crunchy crustaceans (like shrimp). Chinook and coho lick their lips when they see smaller fish and squid. (The disagreeable part for the salmon is they're also on the *receiving* end of teeth: they are snacks for seals, pollock, tuna and sharks.)

A year passes. Maybe even seven years. Then a mysterious signal hits all the fish that hatched in the same place and time: a homing instinct overpowers them. They are compelled to find their home river and return to their hatch-out place. (Each group of salmon that migrates together is called a "run" or "stock.") No one knows how they find their way back. Theories range from smell to stellar navigation. Whatever it is, it works 100 percent.

By the time they get to the mouth of their home river, the fish have put on sexier colours (from silver to red, for the sockeye). The jaws of the males have grown longer; their canine teeth have extended into fierce-looking but useless fangs that stop them from closing their mouths. But it doesn't matter, because when the fish reach fresh water, they stop eating anyway — both male and female — and start living on stored fat. Right away, certain fated and heavy problems begin: they have to fight their way up rapids, around rocks and fallen logs, past hungry and skilful bears, eagles, ospreys, and keep doing all this for maybe hundreds of miles (even more than a thousand). The sorry result is they get to their birthplace in bad shape — gaunt, often with grotesquely humped backs, torn fins, and white patches of bruised skin. (Despite that, the female doesn't indicate "Not tonight, dear.")

But all this is perfect for fish eaters

For ravenous protein-eating humans, salmon are perfect: a fish that goes out in the ocean and eats stuff we can't (plankton) or usually don't want to (tiny herring). They graze in the great North Pacific, grow big with tasty salmon-flesh, then come back as self-propelled packets, in a predictable way, right up streams where they're easy to catch. (You never get diseased ones either, because those die at sea.) You can catch 50 percent of them and not hurt the stock at all. The other 50 percent breed enough new fish to get your numbers back. So mankind couldn't have designed this system better (though government departments do try).

Which means the missing salmon died — they didn't go somewhere else

That lowdown on the salmon cycle sorts out the "duh" question: Have the missing salmon moved to some other rivers, even rivers in another country? No! Their genes don't allow it. If the salmon numbers have dropped for a particular river, those salmon have died out. Even if you put a barrier across a river, the salmon going up the river never shrug and try some other river. They exhaust themselves trying to get past the barrier, and die.

Their relentless homing instinct provides missing-salmon detectives with some other vital information. Their instinct implies it's hard to be sure about their abundance *in general*. Even if you know everything about one river, you monitor it all the time, you watch the salmon numbers increase or fall away over the years, you *can't* say: right, now we know what's happening in all the rivers! Because each salmon run is independent. If a run dies because its river gets poisoned by a pulp mill, or a dam is thrown across it, or the whole salmon run gets netted by seiners at the mouth of the river, then we still know zilch about salmon in other rivers.

Well, what *do* we know about the rivers? That's the place to look. And the river to start with is the biggest — the Fraser River.

The salmon and data that come from the Fraser River

The Fraser River is a whopper. Its salmon runs are big (or they should be). The *catch* used to be as high as 50 million sockeye a year. (Pink and other sorts probably doubled that figure.) That's an educated estimate from 1913. Then a railway was built through the Fraser Canyon. The blasting and excavation set off avalanches that narrowed the river and made a rapid there. The fish couldn't get up it, and that wrecked salmon runs for more than 30 years. Finally in 1944 a "fishway" was built. It looks like a deep ditch, sliced into hard rock, with water flowing down at an easy pace. There's a grate on top — for safety, and so tourists can look down and see the salmon swimming up. (I know about this fishway. My brother Henry helped build it.)

Thanks to that fishway, the sockeye numbers came back, or partly. It happened at a dawdling pace — slowly increasing for 50 years. Oddly, only the sockeye came back in any numbers. What happened to the pink and the others? No one knows. Most people don't realize that any fish are missing — including multitudes who work at the Department of Fisheries and Oceans.

By 1995, there were 20–25 million sockeye coming up the Fraser. Then another man-made catastrophe was wrought upon the fish. The Department of Fisheries and Oceans had been allowing commercial fisheries at the bottom of the river to catch 70 percent of the "spawners" (the salmon that head back upstream to breed). That 70 percent catch was risky, in my judgment. It should have been more like 50 percent. Anyway, here were 70 percent plucked out at the bottom. Then the Department suddenly allowed commercial Indian fishing further upstream. (The reasons they gave for doing that blossom into another story — but it's not important here.)

So where *have* all the fishes gone, long time passing? In 1998, the Fraser catch was down to 3 million, from 25 million before that! Those millions of *missing* fish supposedly died because of higher-than-usual river temperature — that's the official story. If so, then 22 million dead fish should have floated down to Vancouver and created a stink no one could have missed. But they appeared not, neither did they stink.

The Department of Fisheries and Oceans again slammed on the fish brakes: no doing this; no doing that! They now plan for a stable catch of 12 million. That's with a run of maybe 15 million. So they're allowing maybe 3 million spawners to complete their breeding cycle. *This is lunacy!* Here's a river where there was once a *catch* of 50 million sockeye. (And there's an official — if buried — Department figure, by the way, which their sunny scientists quoted to fishing representatives like me: the Fraser has spawning room for 100 million fish.) If anyone remembers that 100 million, they don't draw the compelling conclusion: *No* fishing should be allowed until 30 or 40 million spawners are getting through. That river should be revving along at 100 million fish, not a sputtering 15 million.

After that paragraph, I need to release some steam by making an announcement: From here on in this book, I'm shortening "Department of Fisheries and Oceans" to "DFO." Mentioning the DFO is unavoidable in this tragedy, and I want to reduce their name to a manageable pellet.

Lifeless rivers

That was a swift history of the Fraser River. Not a bright picture, but at least *some* fish still swim there. And the other rivers? We know one thing: nothing can be guessed by gazing at the fish in the Fraser. Yet the DFO does exactly that. It uses the mighty Fraser as the chief indicator for all the river salmon! The Fraser even has an automatic, electronic fish-counter. (The same for the Skeena River — the other river used as an indicator.) The electronic counter is way up the river, past all the fishing. The DFO assumes that the salmon that make it past the fence will also spawn. (That part sounds right.) Unfortunately they then introduced a massive and unregulated commercial fishery *upstream from the counter.*

Meanwhile, for all the other rivers in British Columbia (about 2,000), there are *no* figures. Fishery officers once walked most of them in the fall of each year and estimated the number of spawners. That stopped in the early 1990s. The DFO said it no longer had the budget for it (with a budget 100 times bigger than when fishery officers walked the rivers back in the 1950s).

It *is* still possible to find individuals who can tell you what a certain river used to be like — old-timers, who shake their heads. Ron McLeod, former head of DFO for British Columbia, who had worked his way up from a fishery officer in gumboots, posts to email discussion groups and mourns the collapse of the salmon stocks in Rivers Inlet, for example. That happens to be a place my dad used to fish. In the 1930s, one boat could catch a million salmon a year there, enough to monopolize a whole cannery. Now the stocks are down to three or four thousand spawners.

My dad's logbooks from the 1920s and 1930s noted he was catching sockeye in the saltwater lakes on Vancouver Island in May. In May! I couldn't take that in. These days there aren't *any* sockeye in the whole of British Columbia until late August.

I showed Henry the logbooks: "What the hell is this?"

"Yeah, there was a run of sockeye that used to stay in the salt-water lake. Dad could go in there in the spring and get them. There were several runs like that."

When I talked to the DFO about it, they found no record of those fish. (They seem to know more about fish 100 million years ago.)

When the white settlers arrived in British Columbia, all the rivers were jumping with salmon. Most rivers still thrived until the 1960s. But no more. Ask a fly-fisherman. Ask any bear.

Here's what still needs explaining: Why did the small rivers die, when the Fraser and Skeena didn't quite die? Consider this thought-experiment. Imagine that ocean and coastal fishing took 20 percent of 15 million sockeye that were heading for the Fraser. (That's for illustration; 20 percent isn't meant to be a real figure.) For a smaller river, it might *not* be 20 percent of the run that gets caught. Why? Because if it's a minor river that only has 30 fish going up it, fishermen could catch them *all*, just by chance. You don't believe it? Then think about the most extreme example. Say the number of fish in a certain run is just *two:* one male, one fe-male. You can't catch 20 percent of two fish. Both fish may sneak by you, or you catch one or the other, or catch both. Those are the only possibilities. It means that one year you're *sure* to wipe that run out. From then on, it will be *zero*. The same for a run of 10 fish, or even 50. It just gets more unlikely to wipe them all out in the same year, the more you start with. Yet it's always possible. And almost inevitable for smaller numbers, if you keep at it. A few less each year, then zero. (Like innocent young ducks that keep crossing and recrossing a highway.)

That explains why the little rivers are empty. For certain groups of rivers, scientists saw it coming and said how to avoid it. They wrote reports. They made a noise. And they were ignored. So those rivers died. It's on the record.

The view from space

We now need to increase our altitude; we need perspective, we need to get high enough to see the curvature of the Earth and the larger patterns between things. Then we can finally see what happened to the salmon in British Columbia.

The first fact that splats us in the eye is this: It isn't just Canadian *salmon* that have declined. No! The suspicious thing is that *every* type of fish managed by the DFO has collapsed. This causes wild men to shout: "Idiots! You DFO idiots were managing this and it collapsed! It's your fucking fault!"

Understandable feeling, but the logic isn't perfect. Maybe the DFO did everything they could, maybe no one could have managed things better, and the fish disappeared for reasons that were beyond DFO control. Maybe the fish disappearance would have been *faster* without the skilful work of the DFO. It's possible, right?

Maybe. But consider this additional sign: The few types of fish the DFO *hasn't* managed have done great. Like the halibut. They're managed by the Canadian-American Halibut Commission I mentioned in the last chapter. It's independent of the DFO. Another example is the geoduck (pronounced "gooey duck"). These are large clams, not ducks. Also, their meat isn't gooey. It's choice and prized in China. And they pay a lot for it.

The DFO doesn't "manage" geoducks, and the clams and fishermen have both thrived. There's also a third example (black cod), but I want to save that for later and explain it fully. But it's the same story: The DFO left it alone and it's doing just fine.

So there has to be a suspicion that something's wrong with the DFO management of those fish stocks that collapsed. *But how could people sitting at desks kill all those fish?* I'm now ready to suggest an explanation. This gets intricate, and it's easier to follow if you've seen some episodes of the British television sitcom Yes, Minister (later called Yes, Prime Minister).

First, wince at this: The DFO budget for a fish stock seems to rise the fastest when the fish disappear the fastest. (Zounds! A new law of nature: *As the DFO budget for a fish stock increases, that fish stock decreases.*) It's like that Yes, Minister episode where the health bureaucracy builds a magnificent hospital, crowded with extravagant medical equipment, computer networks, and bustling administrators. Then a question comes up: Why aren't there any patients? Oh, there's no money for *patients!*

So let's consider that the DFO bloated up because of the natural workings of bureaucracy. It's well known why bureaucracy expands. Here are ordinary people, doing their jobs, but each department wants more budget, the junior workers would like to have assistants, the senior staff would like even more staff in order to command even bigger budgets and therefore do their tasks more fully.

That seems to be what happened. People who used to work at the DFO told me about it. First a small division is established to look after, say, salmon. The staff settle in, sort out who sits where, and soon realize they could do much more for the fish if they just had more budget — there are so few people to look after so many fish! The manager of the new Salmon Division feels those pangs acutely. He fights for extra budget and gradually gets it. The Salmon Division expands. As it does, it gains a more commanding voice in DFO affairs. It impresses outsiders from other DFO groups. (All that money — they must be doing more than we are!) Which makes it plausible that the Salmon Division needs even *more* money.

This expansion sucks up human energy. It's an intense experience for the whole staff, a whirl of organization that revels in its own existence, with no time for second thoughts — even if there are fewer and fewer salmon out there (for some reason). In fact, the fewer the salmon, the more budget is needed to save them! This desk-growth could go on and on until the Salmon Division costs more to run than Disneyland, even with no fish left. It's now close to that, with $100 million being spent in British Columbia to manage the salmon, and our percentage of the world catch now one-fifteenth of what it was just 20 years ago.

Ah, but this still doesn't *prove* the DFO caused the salmon decline. After all, it's possible to reason in the following ungainly way: as the Salmon Division grew, it became more and more inward-looking, less and less effective in the real world, and because it meddled less with the fishermen, that actually helped the salmon situation. The DFO uselessness was either *beneficial* to salmon, or did no harm — and the salmon declined for reasons not yet determined. (You can see I'm trying to be fair.)

To get any further, I have to sneak you inside the DFO. I'm able to do this, because over the years I was head of three different fishermen's associations and knew lots of people at the DFO. I argued there at meetings (my honest seagoing face underscored my points), I prowled the corridors, I listened to gossip, I comforted the weeping. Knowing all that, I can tackle that Big Question: *How can they kill fish, sitting at desks?*

1. DFO managers dodge tough decisions, usually out of political timidity

For example, in the early 1990s DFO scientists kept warning about a coho peril. The gist of it was that seine fishing for Fraser sockeye in the Gulf of Georgia and Johnstone Straight was also randomly grabbing parts of the small coho runs heading up the little rivers. Every year the coho were being whittled down. In time, they'd disappear. One way to save the coho would be to cut the sockeye catch in the Gulf of Georgia and Johnstone Straight. Or not catch sockeye at all until they got to the Fraser River. That advice was ignored. It was defeated by the political power of the large fishing-fleet groups that were catching the sockeye. The coho died out.

Another example: the cod fishing off the Grand Banks. The fleets had been catching 300,000 tons a year, but it suddenly proved impossible to catch that much. So the quota was lowered to 200,000 tons, but soon that couldn't be caught either. A scientific report boomed that the stocks were collapsing. It insisted the quota should immediately be cut to 20,000 tons (at most 30,000 tons). The DFO managers groaned they couldn't do that, because *it would put too many people out of work*. (Politics again.) So they left the quota at 200,000 tons. The cod died so fast it amazed everyone (except the scientists). All cod fishing stopped and 40,000 people lost their jobs.

It wasn't just overfishing that slaughtered the cod. The whole fishing method had changed. When the Portuguese were catching Canadian cod 400 years ago, they fished in summer and close to shore. (The cod fed near shore in the summer.) In the winter, the cod took off to the Grand Banks, about 200 miles out, and they spawned there. For almost 400 years, no one fished cod in the winter or on their spawning grounds. But in the 1950s, foreign fleets started doing that. The foreigners were stopped in 1977 when Canada got a 200-mile limit. But then Canadians started fishing on the spawning grounds! And built swaggering fleets of draggers. So the fishing had changed from open-line boats, fishing in the summer near the beach, to dragging year-round, including the spawning season and *on the spawning grounds*. It all happened because it was too hard for the DFO to say no.

2. The DFO often cold-shoulders its own scientific studies

If a DFO scientific report urges some decisive action, it's likely to get smothered. First the report is reviewed by a local fisheries-management group. They write their opinions about it. They may even say: Yes, this is right — we should do it. They pile their opinions on top of the original report and bundle it off to the Pacific Management people in DFO. They place it on their incoming heap, and eventually get around to pondering it. The people who ponder resonate with high-level vibrations that are tuned to DFO politics. What consideration has been taken about the concerns of native people? What will the fishing-fleet owners think of it? How will it go down with the Minister? All these matters and many more are noted, and obscurely translated into DFO-speak. This wordy and baffling output dilutes the strength of the original report (sometimes to an undetectable homeopathic trace). Also, this politically-astute review group probably used the original report in a bid to increase its own budget. Maybe by recommending more research (to be done by their own people). The massive bulk of paper then makes its way to Ottawa and the Pacific Division. It passes before the wary scrutiny of five or six top people. They each *have* to make their own comments on it, because if they don't, they might as well not exist.

By the time this massive missive reaches the Minister (*if* it does), it's not easy to find the original report in all the paperwork that overpads it. It is cushioned with layers of soft iffiness, strapped around the original report like the padded jacket on a dangerous lunatic. So the Minister glances at the top few sheets of this exhausting DFO production. Probably with a languid and self-possessed air, he does the sane thing: Oh, increase the science budget a bit. Or maybe do nothing. (He may only have a year left as Minister, why start trouble?) Certainly *no one* does anything about the report's original recommendation, which may have been modest, practical and important to some local river or fishery.

3. The DFO doesn't reward the right things or punish the right things

I said that 40,000 people lost their jobs because of the cod-fishing collapse. None of those lost jobs were in the DFO. "External" flops like that aren't punished.

On the other hand, success — the sort that matters to people trying to catch real fish — is almost dangerous to DFO employees. I knew persistent individuals in the DFO who managed to increase certain salmon runs. They won no acknowledgment.

There's DFO anxiety about boosting the fish stocks, because it brings hassles about allocating the extra fish. Every fisherman and fleet would start squabbling and demanding and lobbying — an unacceptable hardship for top DFO decision-makers. It's more orderly to look after fish stocks that stay steady, or even decline in a sensible way. And simplest of all, *no* stocks! Bliss it is to manage a well-funded DFO department with no more fish. You think it's impossible?

4. Honest souls grow dejected

The system crunches bold and upright honesty. DFO staff have sighed to me for years about that. They say: See that eager new employee? He's trying hard, but he'll be ground down too. He's putting everything into a path-breaking report. His eyes show fire, he moves briskly, he stays late. But his report is sure to be obliterated in the all-devouring review process. After two or three repetitions like that, even the strongest spirit gives up. He then spits and leaves the DFO, or stays on with a cracked spirit and joins the grubby grab for more budget. Many stay and try to keep the system going, settling for a quiet and adequate living. Their reports now cater to what their superiors want to hear and they stick with tame projects that can cause no trouble. (No *internal* DFO trouble, that is. External trouble, like ruining a fishing stock — that's no cause for worry.)

5. The divisions are isolated, or act like they are

Each sort of fish eventually gets honoured by its own giant DFO division. Those divisions act like jealous experts with tight white lips, guarding their secrets, and they don't wonder how their own fish might interact with fish from other divisions. How would a cut in the herring catch affect the runs of salmon? No one knows. No one seems to care.

Some of the fish must interact in ways that matter. It seems negligent to ignore it.

6. As the fish decline, the answer is to keep reorganizing

I was at a public meeting where a DFO manager took questions about the salmon decline. The audience was in a bad mood, and loud. The manager yelped that the DFO hadn't "managed the resource well." But there was no reason for anyone to worry, because that department had just completed a successful reorganization!

They've been reorganizing the DFO so long they must regularly cycle back through their old organizational attempts.

Here come the theories, excuses and failed experiments

You won't hear any of that from the DFO. What emerges from their public-relations sluice are theories that put the blame somewhere else. Like the following ones.

Ocean conditions have changed!

This has to be one of the vaguest theories ever proposed to explain any serious matter. It's a favourite of the DFO. It's been radiating monotonously from their organization since the early 1990s. It goes like this: There's some unknown force in the Pacific Ocean, some impalpable influence, some undetected change in temperature, a different swirl to the currents, some unknown Factor X out there in the deeps, that's killing our delightful fish before they come back to spawn. That has to be it.

Uh-huh. Except that Factor X has never been pinpointed. Here's another snag: the salmon from Alaskan rivers swim in the same Pacific Ocean as Canadian salmon, but Alaskan stocks have boomed while Canada's have collapsed. The DFO never liked to discuss that startling anomaly with me. How come Factor X affects only Canadian fish? I was told: "Oh, Alaskan salmon, that's all going to collapse too." Real soon now? I'm waiting.

We also need to remember that salmon have been around for 100 million years. They have coped with conditions that must have been impressively abnormal at times, including the asteroid collision with Earth that eliminated the dinosaurs (the fish must have felt the whump). But for some reason these well-tested fish are now so rickety that they fall dead in great numbers because of some undetectable factor in the ocean, one that spares identical fish from Alaska. . . . Riiiiight.

There's *way* offshore fishing

Once there was industrial-strength offshore fishing, as I said in the last chapter — fleets of foreign gillnetters in the North Pacific. Canadian fishermen fumed, and banged on the doors of the DFO, pleading for them to complain to Japan and Taiwan through government channels. Because the gillnetters were catching Canadian salmon — they had to be, fishing right where our salmon cruised and fattened. But the DFO only stared and swayed. When official words came forth, it was to explain to Canadians that the matter was out of their hands, way out in those international waters.

American environmentalists finally clobbered the gillnetters. (Environmentalists seem so astute and balanced when they're on your side.) True, they weren't greatly concerned about the salmon. But they sure didn't like the photos of birds and dolphins trapped in gillnets. So the environmental troops raised a hullabaloo at the UN, and then got going on boycotting Japanese and Taiwanese manufactured goods. The reaction in Japan and Taiwan was satisfactory. No, not our cars! Not our electronics! Exports had suddenly become endangered. So the gillnetters received a message. And they stopped.

Therefore this particular theory — that "way offshore" fishing explains the missing salmon — has now been mushed into another soft and unverifiable Factor X. Because what unmonitored and sneaky fishers could be left out there in the ocean, taking away those missing fish? UFOs with drag nets? The Flying Dutchman?

The rivers have heated up or grown polluted

True, some Canadian rivers have changed: they aren't fed strictly from native rainforests any more, but partly from runoff that gurgles through concrete-covered industrial areas, or towns.

That's probably heated the water and slung in some pollution. It's a fact that pulp mills have polluted certain rivers.

Now let's bring in Alaska. Fasten your logic belts, because I'm going to apply pure reason. Those same undesirable heating and polluting things have happened a lot *less* in Alaska's rivers (because it hasn't industrialized much). So we have a place to compare with British Columbia. The argument is like an example of Mr. Spock's foolproof Vulcan logic: (1) British Columbia's rivers are now hotter and more polluted, and our salmon have declined; (2) Alaska's rivers haven't changed, and their salmon haven't declined; so (3) conclusion: "Isn't it obvious, Captain, that unless there are other factors not yet considered, we may conclude that heat and pollution *have* harmed the salmon in British Columbia's rivers?"

Except there *are* other factors. Coming up!

Before this, we didn't have the technology to kill everything

I've described a modern fishing boat. It's lethal. If fish are out there, they will be found, and when they are found, they will be caught. Even if they're hiding in a coral bed. This is a formidable power and it's new — in the last few decades. There's now the capacity, given enough boats, to exterminate whole fishing stocks.

The DFO claims this is a decisive reason for them to control all the fishing. Because if it was left to the fishermen, it would be like putting the cat in charge of the mice. Nope! Not if the cat has sense. It wouldn't kill all the mice and starve. It would let some of them breed, to keep enough meals scurrying around. And that's what does happens (the "smart cat" theory), in the few cases where fishermen are in charge of their fish stocks. (Proof comes later in this book.) Meanwhile, it's clear that putting all this lethal fishing power in the hands of the DFO hasn't exactly been a success.

The hatcheries will save us

Hundreds of dams were thrown across rivers in Washington and Oregon. The salmon runs for those rivers crashed (a lot like our runs have). But at least the Americans got electricity, even if they lost their salmon. Our salmon stocks crashed and we got nothing but bigger government departments.

When a dam spans a river, some salmon can't get back upriver to their spawning grounds. Even if they can (because of a fishway), the young fish can be sucked into turbines on the way back down, and minced. In the 1950s and 1960s, the Americans tried to make up the numbers by building hatcheries — buildings and "services" in the spawning areas that aimed to boost the breeding rate. Instead of allowing wasteful nature to squander eggs and sperm (because the two don't always get together — sperm swept downstream, etc.), nimble technicians made sure the eggs and sperm were well mixed, and it happened in quiet breeding places that almost resembled labs. And it worked. Instead of maybe 10 percent of eggs becoming fertilized and hatching young fish, the triumph rate went up to 90 percent.

Inspired by these advanced proceedings and not wanting to be outdone, the DFO started building hatcheries too. At last, something better than nature! True, there were very few dams on Canadian rivers, but what the hell! Canada couldn't be left behind in these sex-aids for fish. The DFO called this effort the Salmonid Enhancement Program, which they may have regretted later when the laughter started. (The DFO sex-research program continues and has broadened to human sex. The Calgary *Herald* reported on 24 April 2000 that *"On average, there were about seven visits every day to sex and dating web sites for each of the department's 10,000 staff."* That's right: 70,000 sex visits per day!)

In time, the American hatchery projects failed, or fell so far below hopes or projections that staff spirit drooped in sympathy.

The same happened in Canada. It became clear that nature was not to be mocked. By looking after the fertilized eggs with such care, and then pampering the young fish, it meant that a lot of fish may have survived that ordinarily wouldn't have. The young fish were almost hand-fed in their cozy ponds. They didn't have to forage, but they may have needed that rough experience to learn how to do it. After about ten of these "enhanced" breeding seasons, with fewer spawners coming back each time, the spawners dropped to almost zero. At first, this only stimulated further DFO exertion: in one bold effort, they took the young fish to the ocean *by barge,* to spare them the hazards of going downstream. None of those fish came back. (Maybe they couldn't find the barge.)

Hatcheries in Alaska and Japan

In Alaska, salmon have an easier life. Which again makes Alaska useful for comparison — a kind of control group of one. First, they have only 32 dams that generate electricity. (There are more dams on some *rivers* in northwest America.) And when Alaskans started experimenting with hatcheries, they concentrated on giving nature subtle assistance, instead of trying to take over and boss the whole process. They built "spawning channels" — quiet watery places with some clean gravel. They nurtured only *chum,* because those fish swim straight into the ocean, almost as soon as they hatch. Four years later the chum come back, big and delicious. The Alaskan government allows their fishermen to catch 50 percent of the returning chum. (Patrol boats run along the coast, deterring foreign poachers.) The other 50 percent of the chum are free to spawn. It's a simple system to manage. Nothing to it! You should see the results (data in a minute).

Alaska came to this slowly. They overfished like anything in the 1940s and early 1950s. Easy to do, because of the predictable habits of salmon. It doesn't take much to kill them off. Alaska was down to a catch of a few million salmon a year — close to zero, compared to their historical abundance. The Governor of Alaska erupted with force and speed. He shut the commercial fishery. Not only that, he did a daring thing: he prohibited *any* privileged group from grabbing any of the salmon. He axed the whole native salmon fishery and obliterated the sports fishery. No one was allowed to take a single salmon for about a decade. He also outlawed salmon farms (because of sober worries about their diseases oozing out to the natural runs).

As a positive act, he encouraged fishing groups to build spawning channels and gave them some government money. Then he turned the fishing management over to local groups — management councils of fishermen, fish processors, scientists, and others who want to pipe up. They have open meetings and thrash things out in public.

Result: The Alaskan salmon runs did recover. Their average catch is now well over 100 million a year. Up from just a few million!

Another slamming comparison with Canada comes from distant Hokkaido, in northern Japan. They too build hatcheries for chum, and their salmon catch every year has *always* been more than Canada's. Even though the spawning area in Japan is paltry. Local Japanese fishing communities look after the chum hatcheries. They control their own fish. They *want* fish coming back, thick schools of them, and they bend their common sense and energy to that single-pointed purpose.

Back in Canada

In British Columbia, the hatchery fad faded. A few hatcheries linger, but nothing much comes out of them. In their day, they were a kind of pork barrel converted to a fish barrel — hatcheries were built in "political" areas, not on the biggest rivers or the ones that most needed their fish stocks boosted, but to suit the politics. For prestige. (Vote for Festus Smith, the man who put the salmon hatchery on Goop River.)

Some Canadian spawning channels for sockeye did show perky success rates, but they were run more like labs or university experiments. The DFO program never tried to produce quantities of fish. They didn't count that as success. The idea was to do something impressive. . . . Oh, the contrast to Alaska and Japan.

The legal massacre of salmon and taxpayers

I suspect that most Canadians still think the DFO is doing some good. Alas, it isn't. It subtracts value, like the old Soviet system. More tax money goes into the DFO than the value of goods (fish) that end up in the market.

The DFO used to be slimmer, and may have added value then. But I'm not sure. Anyway, it rolled along like a well-balanced bicycle: it had a practical "gumboot" wheel in the front, and a "data nerd" wheel in the back. Both were needed, and they worked fairly well together. The practical guys in the field needed help with the data, and the data guys needed tips about reality. But these days, the bicycle is ridden by grossly over-weight management, the practical gumboot wheel wobbles badly, and the nerd wheel is dangerously puffed up with hot air. And the managers try to control fishing by remote control, from a long distance.

They've had one strikingly successful policy: cutting the number of fishing boats. For decades, they moaned about too many boats for the number of fish. They never thought of try-ing to increase the number of fish. But they've been victorious in the easier battle of reducing the number of fishing boats (a sad subject I'll come back to). Bureaucratically, it "resolved" the problem. A more complete resolution might be: zero fish and zero boats. We're getting there. The Final Solution for Canadian Fishing.

In one century, we did what once seemed impossible: we killed most of the salmon runs on every river in Canada, from the mighty to the minor. There are 2,000 dispersed rivers, with salmon runs that used to come at different times, so it wasn't easy to kill all that.

In all this, the fishermen did nothing unethical or illegal. (There's been very little poaching.) They followed strict DFO rules and guidelines, and were usually convinced the guidelines were sound. So the salmon stocks have been massacred by "responsible" Canadian government regulation.

The 1999 DFO budget for managing salmon in British Columbia was in excess of $100 million. Yet the salmon fishing brought in only $50 million. Is this intelligent? Doesn't Canada have a smarter use for $100 million than to lose $50 million of it? $50 million would build a well-equipped hospital, to mention one possibility. And one that could afford patients at that.

I've said my piece.

4

Salmon-farm fever

The bright vision

My lament in the last chapter about the missing salmon, the violins I played for them, wasn't it all backward-looking? I barely mentioned the Wave of the Future: *salmon farms*. British Columbia's biggest agricultural export in 1999 was — guess what? — farmed salmon (worth $308 million). So who needs *any* river salmon?

As the wild salmon disappear, the farmed salmon replace them. So that's no problem, right? We still get our salmon to eat. But I'll plant my feet and say this: Salmon farms breed some heavy troubles, and while those troubles can probably be fixed, it will cost a lot. Because of those troubles and costs — which will rise to a scary peak in a few years — Canadians may not be eating a lot of farmed salmon in the year 2030, or 2080, or even 3500.

But let me put aside the troubles for a minute. Instead, I want to show what you might have read in a 1980s investor brochure for some salmon farm. In the brochure text, you could feel the prudent company lawyer struggling against the emotional public-relations writer. Their uneasy joint production typically came out reading something like this:

An investment in Goop Bay Salmon Farm is an investment in the future. Old-fashioned fishing with nets and hooks is dying — this is well known. However, human ingenuity is boundless and has found the solution. What is coming next is a mammoth revolution, as big a revolution as when agriculture began in ancient times. Mankind discovered it didn't need to forage and hunt in the forests, but could plant and harvest in the fields. In the same way, we have now realized that we don't have to *hunt* for fish. We can *breed* them in a controlled farming situation, with high efficiency and great productive yield.

We no longer need to rely on casually trained people who follow an inefficient tradition on boats, but can put our trust and investment in detailed scientific research about how fish breed, grow and are best nourished. That extensive knowledge, increasing all the time, can be put to work in feeding the world, as well as making considerable but ethical profits for our investors. Fish farming is set to become a booming growth industry, perhaps the biggest growth industry in the last few hundred years, maybe as big as industrialization itself, with massive rewards for those who invest early.

Simply consider the payback projection. Laboratory tests have proved that for every pound of cheap but wholesome fish-feed consumed by the farm fish, almost a pound of high-quality marketable salmon flesh is produced. This high conversion efficiency is thought to occur because the farm salmon don't waste energy by having to adjust to different water temperatures, or fight gravity by swimming upstream. A pound of fish feed currently costs about 20 cents, and a pound of salmon sells for as much as $8. The other costs in operating a salmon farm are very low. It is simply a matter of maintaining the pens (to protect the investment salmon from predators, for example), feeding the fish regularly, and monitoring their rapid growth.

Moreover, genetic science is beginning to implement methods to *modify* salmon so they will grow even *faster* in the farm environment, but without losing any meat quality. It is similar to the way generations of farmers learned to breed cattle for better milk yield and meat quality. However, the cattle-breeding process was slow, clumsy and nearly random compared to what is now possible with direct genetic manipulation. Amazing genetic precision is now routine in the laboratory. Many of the experiments with transgenic salmon are already extremely promising.

Considering all this, can you afford *not* to invest in this thriving and rapidly expanding growth industry?

Hey ho! Why didn't we think of this earlier? Sounds as easy as shooting fish in a barrel. In theory, it is. The "pens" are set up in the water along a river, or right on the ocean shore. The sides of the pens are nylon net and each pen is the size of a small swimming pool. A farm has a lot of pens packed together side by side, like square floor tiles, maybe as many as 100 pens. Floating walkways let the farmers get to any pen.

There are lots of pens instead of one big one, because it's not possible to *mix* fish of different ages. The bigger fish would eat the little ones. Even if that didn't happen, it wouldn't be easy to extract just the older fish in a mixed population. So each pen has one cohort of fish, all the same age. The youngest cohort may be a new pen-load of fish straight from the hatchery (the farms usually buy the young fish, and don't try to hatch them from eggs).

The salmon live in the same pen for about four years. Feed snows down from the surface at set times, and the water boils with the flapping and lunging. (By the way, it isn't a precise use of words to call a setup like this a fish "farm." These are fish *feedlots*. But I'll keep calling them "farms" because it's the word everyone now uses.) When the fish are ready to sell, they're usually pumped out through a fat flexible pipe, a kind of underwater vacuum cleaner.

So that's the bright vision about fish farms. Or at least as bright as it gets.

From bright vision to tarnished reality is only a step.

The tarnished reality

In 1983 I met Brad, one of the people who started the salmon-farming business in British Columbia. Radio gossip between our empty salmon boats started mentioning this guy. He had built an experimental salmon farm, it was said, and seemed to know what he was doing. So I phoned him. Right away he invited me to his house to inspect his project.

Brad's house looked out over the salmon farm, with the pens clustered at the edge of a bay. I walked around with him, stared, listened and asked firm questions. Brad was bright, hard-working, animated. He had a pony tail and the sincere intensity found in true believers and path-finders. I might have been walking around with Daniel Boone.

Brad said he got technical help from DFO scientists (who seemed very keen) and he got his small fish from their hatcheries. His wife also laboured at their little salmon farm. They'd both kept outside jobs as social workers to pay the farm expenses, because the fish were tiny, were doing OK, but had years to go.

My brain vibrated with interest and suspicion. It *might* work out, these penned fish, I was thinking. But my dominant investment aim is not to *lose* my money. There were technical snags and perils in this hopeful operation, though I was told these snags would be overcome "real soon." I could also detect financial perils on a bigger scale — brutal killers of profit and business.

I thanked Brad for his time and said I'd like to know how it all worked out. I put in no money.

Brad's little fish farm never did produce marketable fish. But it soon grew into a thriving *financial* business. Stock-market promoters embraced Brad's farm and packed it into a new and empty company. They packed in other leases for other watery locations, to start other fish farms. Brad and his wife were handed millions of shares, the promoters got millions of shares, and the public was offered the rest. Public shares started at $1, then moved energetically upstream to $5, like salmon up a rapid. The owners and the promoters were abrupt millionaires (according to their certificates), so they rented appropriate offices in Vancouver. Brad was sent out to give seminars, as president of the company, to raise even more money for more expansion.

I was still following this, wondering if I'd been right to stay out, and I went to a couple of Brad's investment seminars. He presented himself well, radiated that Daniel Boone honesty, and plainly believed everything he said. The profitability projections looked sensational, the company was packed with investor money, and nothing stood in the way. It was already one of the biggest salmon-farming ventures in British Columbia.

Time passed. The books showed they had millions of fish in their pens. But when it came to *selling* the fish, no one seemed able to find them. Investors rose to shouts of "fraud!" Brad was fired, removed from the commercial world — as if he'd been yanked away by a giant hook — and was impossible to find for interviews. Everyone blamed him for everything, not least the promoters, who toughed out some severe interviews by blaming the disgraced president.

I couldn't tell you if the salmon ever existed in any numbers, or if they did, what happened to them. The one definite thing I saw was the almost lightning-storm energy directed into raising money. Brad was hectic with lectures and promotion, downtown in a suit. Nobody else seemed to know a great deal about raising captive fish. For that matter, Brad had still been learning. So I don't know who was supposed to be minding the pens.

Meanwhile, other Canadian fish farms had started surf-boarding on the investment wave. Fish pens had been set up all over. But as those pioneer years passed, the farms struggled, most collapsed, and a spreading ruination ended in consolidation, with the big fish farms swallowing the little fish farms. Canadian investors lost $300 million and adjusted to a darker image of fish farms.

Most of the fish farms that are left in Canada are owned by corporations that can afford them. Some corporations are Norwegian, because little fish farms in Norway had started before the Canadian craze and they got the knack of producing real fish. Also, the market in those early days took all the salmon the farms in Norway could produce, and at super-profit market prices. But Norwegian law banned anything but family farms, and still does. So to expand and invest their bulging profits, the Norwegians started buying up foreign farms. That's why they came to Canada (among other places).

Today even the big corporate Canadian farms are erratic in their profitability. The corporations try to protect themselves by owning all the businesses involved — the farms, the fish processors, and the supermarkets where the fish are sold. They also have the money to endure hard years, or recover if their penned fish get sick and die. They need those financial advantages. It is still hard going.

If these sober, well-funded, and experienced fish farmers still struggle, what's the trouble?

High costs, low market prices

In that pretend-brochure I wrote at the beginning of this chapter, I said: *Laboratory tests have proven that for every pound of cheap but wholesome fish-feed consumed by the farm fish, almost a pound of high-quality marketable salmon flesh is produced.* That's a 1:1 ratio of fish food to salmon meat. Too bad it didn't turn out that way in the fish farms.

Part of the feed settled to the bottom and rotted. Some drifted with currents, out of the pens. And maybe the conversion ratio could *never* be that wonderful anyhow in a real pen (compared to a spotless laboratory, where the ideal ratio was measured). The real conversion figure is about *four* pounds of fish-feed to *one* pound of farmed salmon (a poor 4:1 ratio, not a rich 1:1).

It gets worse. That protein feed comes from third-world countries, mainly South American countries like Chile. They catch billions of sardines and anchovies, and transmute them into fish-food pellets. They use the pellets in their own salmon farms (yeah, they're into this too). And they sell their surplus pellets. So far the world price of the pellets has been constrained, if rising. But you see the problem: What if too many fish farmers want those pellets? The pellet price will go up faster, crushing the feeble profit curves of the farms. That's been happening. And if the price of feed jolted up by a sudden 25 percent or 50 percent, the fish farmers would still have to pay. No choice. They can't let their fish starve.

It gets worse. Those third-world countries don't look after their fishing stocks as well as they could. (To make the most diplomatic sort of comment I'm capable of.) They may soon overproduce and *wipe out* the source of those cheap pellet supplies. No more pellets for anyone! Which is why there's panicky Canadian research to find something *else* to feed salmon. Soy protein. Grains. Anything!

The DFO pays for some alternative-feed studies (but why,

considering their mandate is to look after the *wild* fish stocks?).
At first the disgusted experimental salmon got sick on the soy and
grain mixtures, lost hope, and died. Not surprising. In the last 100
million years, those were the only salmon presented with such a
diet. Researchers recently got the experimental salmon to eat
some vegetable feed and not show their displeasure by dying. The
DFO added a dash of fish protein, so the salmon liked the taste
better. But it's a long way from a few queasy and reluctant salmon
to commercial production and contented salmon. The labs are
also tinkering with salmon genetically, so they might live on
grains, like cattle, and even enjoy it. (What might we call these
grain-loving fish — "prairie salmon"?)

One place where salmon farms could go on thriving for a
while is Chile. After all, they supply the pellets and set the price
for them. They have cheap labour. And they don't have wild
salmon around that might spread diseases into their tame-
salmon pens. The Chilean farmers are also spared a lot of environmental rules, because few exist. So that's another cost that
isn't weighing on them.

That was the hard news about *costs*. Salmon from the Canadian farms started off costing maybe $2 a pound to produce
(thanks to those cheap pellets). That cost is a $2 weight in the left-
hand pan of the profit balance. The pan on the other side weighs
the market *price* for the salmon. It used to be high, $6–$8 a pound,
back when there were only wild salmon and a few insignificant
fish farms. You could produce salmon at $2 a pound and sell it at
$8. No wonder investors shouted "I'm in!"

What happened next might have been predicted by old hands
who knew about the pig cycle. With pigs, a high market price
brings forth overproduction, following the human laws of greed
and hope. Ditto with salmon. Marketable salmon were eventually
vacuumed from the farm pens in great abundance. So the price for

all salmon fell, and fell, and fell. The best salmon now sell for 60–80 cents a pound (down a tad from $8 a pound, right?). The pinks go for 15 cents a pound, and that's good-quality fish.

I knew about the pig cycle, but for some reason I didn't see how overpowering the salmon glut might be. As fishermen, we were so used to salmon as a *demand* market, one that was hard to fill. Now it's oversupplied. No one makes much money, least of all people still catching the wild salmon — even in Alaska. The salmon farms struggle, and make a little profit when they hit the market cycle at the right spot (that is, they have fish to supply when the market price is temporarily up).

Well, what's wrong with all that? Consumers get superb fish at low cost. (OK, maybe not superb. Farm salmon taste milder than wild fish, but quite close to seined fish.) But you can sense the risks in relying on farmed fish. The supply of pellet food is one risk. Further crashing and elimination of the wild fisheries because of low salmon prices is another. And there are other problems.

Pollution

Pollution? What pollution? These are salmon in their natural element, water — confined in pens, OK, but doing their usual things, with currents sweeping through and keeping things clean. That's what I used to think — that pollution was environmental hysteria. Until some evidence sludged my way.

"Bert" dives for geoducks. He told me the sea bottom is killed for about a *mile* around each fish farm. Dead. The fish food and poop that drifts out seems to overload the bottom with nutrient. That unnatural load acts like poison. (That's a vague and medieval explanation, but it's the best we have. The DFO doesn't even research this.)

I asked other divers. Bert was right — the same dead scene

stretched around any fish farm *any* diver had seen. That makes sense if you've had a ground-zero look at a feedlot operation on land — let's say hogs. The smell. The ooze. The *horror*. It has to be that way with fish farms, only submerged and somewhat hidden. Whether you pack 1,000 hogs in a small area or 1,000 fish in small pens, there must be bad effects.

Higher-level data is now available. It has been revealed that British Columbia's fish farms, acting together, expel the same tonnage of raw sewage as a city of half a million — if a city that size dumped *raw* sewage (and some Canadian cities do that).

To end this informative bottom-up discussion, and give it a higher tone, here are two academic quotes:

> *BC's salmon industry uses publicly owned coastal waters to support intensive private feedlot operations that raise carnivorous species and dump drug-laced sewage into the ocean. Governments hoping for new economic opportunities in coastal areas have encouraged the industry. But any benefits are more than offset by an alarming array of environmental, health, social and economic costs.*
>
> — from the David Suzuki Foundation website

And more abstractly and broadly, but with the full punch of a heavy-weight scientific journal:

> *The increasingly large scale of these industries, combined with other human activities, now places substantial demands on ocean ecosystems, which in turn result in the demise of [wild] fisheries and biological diversity. These ecological impacts are not reflected in either local or international prices for aquaculture inputs or outputs. So long as the full environmental costs of feed and stock inputs, effluent assimi-*

lation, and coastal land conversion are not recognized in the market, ocean resources — including [wild] fisheries — will deteriorate further.

— Naylor, Raymond, et al., *Science*, Vol. 282, October 1998.

Ugh. OK, there's a pollution problem.

Diseases and antibiotics

If one fish in a feedlot pen gets a sniffle, all fish in the farm get it. And some fish diseases are fatal — farmers lose every fish. The diseases often have names that sound like witch curses: *Laxanaemia* or *Furunculosis*. Fish wipeouts have happened on a plague scale in Norway, Scotland, and Eastern Canada.

Alaska banned fish farming because of this disease dread. But the Alaskans were looking at this from the wild-fish side: they didn't want epidemics spreading from the farm fish to their wild stocks (the wild fish are still doing fine, as I've said a few times).

Meanwhile, Canadian fish farmers fight disease in the no-nonsense feedlot tradition. They use antibiotics. ("Tip in more drums there, Mario. They're not looking so good.") Fish farms absorb more antibiotics per pound of meat output than any other farming, including those overdosed chickens we all hear about. The same sorts of antibiotics go into the salmon pens as the anti-biotics used to treat sickly humans in hospital beds. Everyone knows it's mad to give bacteria a head start in feedlots, where they can mutate into antibiotic-resistant killers that afflict good-natured people like you and me. The fish-farm meat may even have *pure* antibiotics left in it, and you chomp right into that too. Then you can breed your own drug-resistant bacteria.

Fish farmers have probably received a DFO rule sheet about antibiotics, but they know the rules are slackly enforced. When the fish in their pens look green about the gills, the farm worker may look left, look right, and heave in even more antibiotics. (I've heard about that, but haven't seen it happen myself.)

What's the answer? Even if squads of "antibiotics police" took away random samples of fish, raided pens at night with searchlights and managed to stop all recklessness, would the DFO be satisfied with the result? Mass death in the fish pens? Not an easy one.

Hazards to the wild salmon

Fish plagues

I've said that Alaska didn't want fish farms to infect their wild fish. You might think: Hey, come on, don't the penned ones carry the same diseases as the wild ones? Not necessarily. Because there's a peculiarity about the farm salmon. They are mostly Atlantic salmon, not found in waters around British Columbia or anywhere in the Pacific (sort of obvious, with a name like Atlantic). But Atlantic salmon are the darlings of salmon farmers, because the fish are placid as well-groomed cows. The Atlantic salmon are satisfied to be in pens and looked after. Definitely not true of sockeye and other belligerent Canadian salmon — they fight to get out, and never stop struggling (somewhat similar to Canadian taxpayers).

The point is this: The Atlantic salmon might carry diseases, might arrive with diseases they're almost immune to themselves, but which can kill populations of Pacific fish. (Like Columbus and his germy crew accidentally killing eight million welcoming natives of Hispaniola.) Atlantic salmon have already done that to wild-fish stocks in Scotland and Norway. Other wild-fish epidemics were spread in New Brunswick and Ireland. But not yet in British Columbia.

Eat not thy wild neighbour

Except for spreading diseases, what else could penned fish

possibly do to harm the free-ranging native ones? (It's a bit like that question about the DFO: What could those penned-up officials possibly be doing that could kill fish?)

Here's one possibility (for the open-minded): the penned fish might *eat* the wild fish. What is this, you wonder, one of Eric's little jokes? But imagine if *small* wild fish swim into those pens. There may be big fish in there (between meals, craving a snack). I've said how the water seems to boil when food is thrown in. So it's possible that little wild fish might get eaten. You protest: but surely not *many* of the wild fish! Consider the endless oceans, the smallish pens, and the way the genes of the free salmon propel the little fish out to sea — not take them into coastal pens.

Here's why: the fish farmers leave bright lights on at night. Their notion is to eliminate the difference between day and night and keep the fish awake and feeding. I have no idea if that works, but fish farmers believe it. What I *do* know from experience is that some fish are powerfully lured by bright lights. So powerfully lured that lights have been outlawed as a way to catch those fish. It works too well and fish stocks can be annihilated. See what I'm saying? Those fish-farm lights could be pulling schools of little salmon into those pens at night. Then chomp . . . Gone.

Let me illustrate. Back in the 1970s, when I was working on my brother Henry's boat, we used to catch herring using lights. We'd anchor in a bay, rig up some streetlights on the boat and leave them on all night (it's called "pit lamping," from a sly procedure that hunters once used to attract deer — wearing miner's pit helmets with lights on them). The streetlights drew little fish from all over the bay. We could see them converge, using our simple fish-finder and riding around in a skiff. The fish packed around the lights. We'd run a seine net around them and pull them in. We needed to catch swarming quantities of them, because herring sold for just $30 a *ton*. If we caught a few hundred tons a week, deck hands like me could still make a decent wage (in those days) of $50 a week.

But the lights didn't just attract herring. We found small salmon in the net, and every other kind of little fish known to live in the bay. (Big fish weren't attracted. I don't know why.) The pit-lamping was so ruthless that fishermen had qualms. There were union meetings and proposals to outlaw the method. We always agonized about any remote possibility of destroying fish stocks, our whole living. But a DFO scientist descended from the mountain and held up a calming hand: "Do not be vexed, brothers, for one herring hath two million eggs, and thus simply by sparing ten tons of quick herring, adequate breeding capacity will remain in order to replicate the numbers and maintain a stable stock."

Right, sport. So pit-lamping went on, but the herring catch strangely declined — despite the DFO prophecy. In the 1970s, fishermen in British Columbia used to catch 300,000 tons of herring a year. With ease. In the decades since then, the price of herring stratosphered from a mere $30 a ton, to as high as $8,000 a ton (because of demand by the Japanese, who see herring as a kind of food for the gods). And guess what? The herring catch is now only 20,000 tons — about 7 percent of what it used to be! So pit-lamping was of course banned. It's now banned almost everywhere, in every country.

Now we can picture a school of young salmon cruising out of the Fraser River, and heading for sea at night. They spot a well-lit fish farm. See what could happen? I don't have proof. But it's worth investigating. Maybe this night illumination should only be allowed in *one* farm, and that farm monitored scrupulously, and a random sample of penned fish opened up regularly to see what they've been eating.

Are you wondering, how can I be sure little fish can really get in, are the net meshes big enough? The answer is yes. There's proof. Some corporate fish farms have officially asked the DFO if they can keep the small — and valuable — black cod that trespass into their pens. (The DFO said yes. More on that intriguing response in a later chapter.) But if small black cod can get in, so can small salmon. Case closed.

One solution is to turn the lights off. Another solution is to require the mesh in the pens to be reduced. Neither solution has been used, or even talked about.

Genetic upheaval

Pit-lamping and fish-farm disease aren't the only threats to wild fish. Bad things can even happen when *healthy* Atlantic salmon break out of the pens and mix with sockeye, chum, chinook, coho, and pink. It doesn't take much of an accident for farm fish to get out — maybe a sea lion chewing holes in the pens. Now and then Canadian newspapers have carried stories about mass breakouts of Atlantic salmon, maybe 100,000 of them suddenly free. About a million Atlantic salmon have escaped into British Columbia's waters so far.

Some Atlantic salmon even *breed* in British Columbia's rivers. This definitely wasn't supposed to happen — even if "a few" did escape from the farms. The DFO claimed that escapees would never be able to work out what to do. For salmon it would be like: "Duh, where's my river?" But with enough escapes, there are always a few salmon geniuses or lucky ones that figure it out and adopt a river. They may even drag along a mate, who follows out of interest. The first live evidence was spotted by a university student doing some cheap research. He was simply walking along a river, using his eyes. And there they were: Atlantic salmon, spawning. (The DFO doesn't walk these rivers, as I said, so how could they have known?) Atlantic salmon have now been found spawning in 30 rivers in British Columbia — and I doubt we've heard the end of the story.

So what? Just this: The last thing the wild stocks need is *another* threat. Atlantic salmon in the rivers might interfere with the spawning of the wild fish. The Atlantics might dig up the wild-salmon eggs, for example, and lay their own. That happens between competing wild salmon — or used to, in those half-forgotten times when there were enough salmon to compete. No one really knows what the effects of the Atlantic salmon may be. It may even be *good* to have Atlantic salmon in the rivers, but there's reason to be cautious here.

Meanwhile, back in the DFO's West Vancouver lab, experiments proceed with thousands of genetically modified Pacific salmon. On 20 Jan 2001, the Calgary *Star* reported that "DFO researchers have now created 20 new genetic lines of salmon which grow approximately five to seven times faster than unaltered fish." The lab has also produced transgenic fish with "enhanced bacterial resistance" and others that give birth to offspring of only one sex.

Those interesting fish have not escaped. Or been provided to fish farmers. Again, I'd say we need to go carefully. It all gives me an eerie feeling, and I refreshed my memory about this part of Francis Bacon's *New Atlantis* (written in 1626):

We find means to make commixtures and copulations of divers kinds, which have produced many new kinds, and them not barren, as the general opinion is. We make a number of kinds of serpents, worms, flies, fishes of putrefaction, whereof some are advanced (in effect) to be perfect creatures, like beasts or birds, and have sexes, and do propagate. Neither do we this by chance, but we know beforehand of what matter and commixture, what kind of those creatures will arise.

We have also particular pools where we make trials upon fishes, as we have said before of beasts and birds.

We are heirs to that long-ago Faustian longing. We can now *do* that stuff. But what has begun?

The missing Omega-3

The easy-going Atlantic salmon in the pens don't have the good muscle tone of the athletic wild fish. That means the farm salmon have a low content of omega-3 — a certain fatty acid that gives some protection against heart disease in humans who eat the fish.

That may seem a minor point. But it's known and verified, and means we might be wary about accepting that farmed fish are equally as nutritious as wild fish. Maybe they are (except for omega-3), maybe not. Better keep our options free and let the wild fish thrive too. We may need them.

Protecting the pens

I've mentioned sea lions biting holes in the pens. It happens. They try to get at the delectable salmon. Dogfish (a small shark) also try, and sometimes succeed. Also seals. To those predators, the salmon pens look like food bars.

This means the fish farmers have to patrol the pens and scare away sharp-toothed creatures that look in hungrily — or shoot them. Unknown numbers of sea lions and seals get shot that way in British Columbia. Environmentalists aren't too pleased. Birds also get caught in the nets, and even whales manage to get tangled up. With all that going on — gunfire, whales thrashing around, the lights — the penned salmon must never get any rest.

Predator problems are normal in old-fashioned land farming. In sunny seeded fields, songbirds become dire pests. If you're going to have any kind of farm, you're going to have a class of creatures that are suddenly called pests and have to be fought or frightened off. But if someone else *likes* the pests and wants them protected, the farmer can face legal ire, not to mention people marching with angry signs about fox bait or rabbit traps. It all comes with the job.

What *is* in those cans of salmon?

People quiz me about the cans of salmon in the supermarkets. They're so cheap! What's in them? Simple: it's always *wild* salmon, for two reasons:

1. Wild salmon is now very cheap. Alaska catches maybe 150 million pink salmon a year, for example, and the fishermen get 20 cents a pound or less. Even with processing, canning, and shipping, a supermarket can of that salmon is indeed cheap. (Farmed salmon can't compete at that price — their fish have to be fed and looked after for years.)

2. The soft muscle texture of farmed salmon rules out canning. Canned fish have to be cooked at a high temperature, and that makes the farmed salmon go mushy. So they wouldn't be used in cans, even if they were cheap enough.

Farmed salmon are sold in the fresh-fish market, or as fresh fish in supermarkets. It's the only place the farmed fish can be sold and get a high enough price to make fish farming pay. So when you buy a fresh or frozen supermarket fish, it may be farmed or it may be a (good-looking) wild one. You can't easily tell.

I should confirm this: the canned fish taste OK, they're healthy eating, and certainly cheap enough. And they're almost always safe, because the meat is cooked long and hot. But be careful about canned salmon from some place like Thailand. Pirates catch salmon in the mid-Pacific and their sneaky catches are sometimes canned in Thailand under conditions that would sicken a micro-biologist.

Political vectors and strong feelings

Let's rise above technicalities and probe the feelings of the people and groups that affect fish farming.

DFO

There's a schizoid gap between what the DFO says about fish farming and what they do. Their official voice declares they want to protect the wild salmon, they are right behind it. That's what the DFO charter says: they're there to look after Canada's *natural* fishing resources (not to promote new industries). But unofficially, signalled by their actions, they seem to favour the fish farms to the wild fish. The traditional fishing industry is a headache for them, with many complexities and things (like fish) that don't always obey government commands. What they seem to be thinking is:

"The wild stocks are obviously declining (something that nature chose to do — we at the DFO couldn't help it). So it's time to get behind something more modern, productive and controllable. Why not eliminate the fishing fleets and those few stray wild fish that might spread disease to the farm fish? It's certainly easier to work with the big corporations that run the big fish farms, compared to struggling to communicate up-to-date ideas to disorderly and backward fishermen. The corporations also give us useful political backing. We can work with our own kind of people, because fish farming needs scientists and other academically trained people."

Notice the binary either/or. We can have wild fish *or* we can have fish farming. I suggest: why not both?

I say the DFO favours fish farming. Evidence isn't hard to find.

In early 2001, the Auditor General of Canada reported that the DFO wasn't "fully meeting its legislative obligations under the Fisheries Act to protect wild Pacific salmon stocks and their habitats from the effects of salmon farming." There were shortfalls in their monitoring, and in their research about the effects of the fish farms. Not only that, they had *no* plan for managing the risks from the farms.

In earlier reports, the Auditor General worried about the DFO's slackness in protecting wild-fish habitats. Wild salmon had fewer and fewer of those. He also frowned about the escape of Atlantic salmon and the extra stress it could put on the wild stocks. If that wasn't bad enough, he pointed out that in 1985 the DFO had drafted rules for siting fish farms but had never enforced them.

I've already said the DFO no longer monitors the smaller rivers. They say they can't afford it. That meant they didn't know that Atlantic salmon were breeding there, until a strolling university student broke the news.

But the DFO *does* find the money to fund research that helps fish farmers, like the genetic work I mentioned earlier. It's like the DFO doesn't have its boots on the right feet.

Fishermen

A lot of fishermen see things something like this:

"The right political move is to stick with the wild salmon, like Alaska did. You don't have any of the bad stuff from fish farming, or don't have to mess around to find solutions for that. Canada is making the wrong choice here. Nature gives a better product, it costs one-tenth as much to harvest as farmed salmon, and you don't even have to whistle for the fish to come home. Anyway, what's the DFO think it's doing, promoting an industry like fish farming that's controlled by big foreign corporations? As much as we do like the Norwegians, the DFO are supposed to be looking after *us*.

"Anyway, fish farming can't work in Canada if they have to sort out all the problems, because that will run their costs up too high. The only reason the farmers don't have those costs now is the DFO *doesn't* enforce its own fish-farming regulations. And don't think that the cheap fish-feed from Chile is going to stay cheap. No way.

"If there weren't any wild fish left, and no hope for them to recover, then OK — we'd have no choice. We could fix the fish-farm problems, or live with them. Sure, there's pollution, but there's more pollution from a pulp mill and we've managed to cope with that. But we still have a choice, so why not at least talk about it? This bias toward farmed salmon seems to have crept in without much discussion at all."

Certain hopeful and well-meaning citizens

The plea from citizens sounds like this:

"We all know the wild salmon have collapsed. We're not sure why, but they had that same problem in Alaska and fixed it by *not* fishing for a long time. Their salmon came back. So the fish farms give us a wonderful chance to do that here in Canada: *Just stop fishing wild salmon, while we all eat farm salmon.* When the wild fish come back, we'll have both types. Perfect."

Environmentalists

This line from the David Suzuki Foundation glumly sums it up: "The combined risks to human health, the environment, native species and the BC economy add up to an industry that is not sustainable."

There are book-loads of analysis and research on the Suzuki website, and I might compress it like this:

"Fish farming can be fixed, and must be fixed. Closed-loop containment systems must be built inland, completely separated from the wild fish, instead of leaky pens in the ocean. Only native salmon must be farmed, not Atlantic, genetically changed, or imported types. Public health must be protected with strict monitoring of antibiotics. The whole industry must have limited public subsidies and the details of those subsidies must be made public and audited. And we must stop using fish-food that could also be used for human food."

Me

I'll include myself as an influence, because I've written this book. Here's what I think:

I suspect that fish farming *isn't* going to be economic in Canada for long. Stricter controls will be put on the farms, and that will rocket up their costs. Even if the whole business isn't forced to move inland and run in hermetically-sealed environmental units, they *will* have to improve things in the coastal pens. Even the mere DFO enforcement of all the rules it's *already* supposed to enforce would send up costs. Meanwhile, there's that thread-hanging risk about the price of cheap fish-food. The price could suddenly rise by a high multiple and stay high. The only answer to that one is to force the penned fish to eat some inexpensive plant food. Not easy.

I suspect that fish farming isn't even going to stay economic in places like Chile. They only have to start caring more about the environmental harm they are causing themselves. But that's not all. Consider the normal cycle of third-world fishing developments: it expands at a searing pace, and then collapses in about a decade. This has happened, to name one example, in Chile with their sea-bass industry. I wait for the same thing to happen with their salmon farms.

There will always be fish farms in certain places. (There were fish farms — of a simple sort — in China in 2,000 BC. So parts of this industry aren't new at all.) And technology may finally fix most of the problems and give these operations a passable profit. There may yet come those well-run, sealed-off farms with fish modified to eat grain, grow fast, and taste great. But that bright reality may stand as far in our future as *New Atlantis* stands in our past.

Meanwhile, let's protect the wild stocks that are left and try to get them back in bigger numbers. Let me put it to you this way. Imagine that pioneer American cattle ranchers knew what a modern rancher knows. Then the *buffalo* would still be around.

It took a long time for cattle to overgraze the grass that had evolved to suit the buffalo. The grass had survived for ages. So had the buffalo. Now those buffalo grazing grounds are all cheatgrass and hardpan. Cattle can't live on it; buffalo can't live on it.

Today's cattle have to be fed on corn fertilized with petrochemicals, a bit like feeding salmon artificially in pens. But the buffalo were like *wild* salmon. They didn't need looking after. They didn't need feeding in the winter. The "herding" was mainly noting where they went. Their meat was choice, and if they were only hunted in moderation, they kept coming back in the same numbers. The ranchers now want the buffalo back, but can't make it happen. There isn't enough money in the world to get rid of the cheatgrass that's spread over 100 million acres.

The newcomers — the cattle — slowly destroyed a natural resource that everyone took for granted. No one understood.

5

Museum notes from a fishing village

Harry was from Texas. He had a whopping allowance from his parents, paid on the condition that he never go back to his home town. He had a Moses beard, which didn't look too clean, and a head that was packed with schemes for world improvement. I met him in San Francisco and I used to listen to him sometimes. Listen, not talk. Because communication was mostly one-way: from Harry to the world. But I now see that certain things he said are true.

We are living, Harry insisted with long-stare intensity, in a *museum*. For example, consider your kitchen. If it could be transported into the far future and put into a museum there, it would attract keen attention.

Harry had stretched his time-museum insight into a whole theology: His church would train its flock to treasure their own surroundings and life, however low and grubby. They would see their lives as a future race might look back on them — incomparable, full of character, and perfect for their time.

True enough. So let me use that Harry approach and guide you through a time-museum of my boyhood village. Because these vanished scenes are part of what this book is about: How Canada moved from fish in abundance, an endless flapping bounty, to scarcity and barrenness.

Panorama

Museum Gallery 1: Bamfield, 1950

Barely 300 people live in Bamfield, about half of them aboriginal people. From a boat on Bamfield Inlet (a body of water called "The Creek"), all their houses can be seen around the shoreline. Steep hills and forest stand behind, with one rugged and prominent massif, like Diamond Head in Hawaii.

Each house has its "float" — a raft-like berth anchored in the water, where a boat can tie up. A ramp of rough planks leads from the float to the land, and sometimes right to the house. The floats rise and fall with the tides, like a kind of moon clock. There are no roads here, and no cars.

The Wickhams' house is privileged to have a dock as well as a float. This dock stands with Swedish firmness on fixed piles. It took three years of cursing labour to build. The family's big seiner, the first one in Bamfield, ties up there.

Behind the Wickhams' house stands the rainforest. Hemlock, balsam, spruce, cedar, fir. Trees of great girth and tonnage. Around The Creek edge, in random stabs, some forest is cleared, or shows past signs of it. Most houses have a small garden. But the forest richness soon leaches away when trees are cleared, and then fish scraps are dug in as fertilizer. Meanwhile, the forest never gives up. Fed by drenching rainfall, it means to win — and it will, if these people slacken at all.

If we could rise straight up for miles (and let's imagine the sky is clear for a change), other villages could be seen along the West Coast of Vancouver Island. Hundreds of them. And hundreds of rivers and streams, spawning places for uncountable salmon.

Museum Gallery 2: Bamfield, 1910

A sweating, hard-breathing man struggles on either end of a

tremendous handsaw, pushing, pulling, pushing, pulling, trying
to cut through a colossal tree. One is my dad, a new arrival from
Sweden. The other is his one-eyed brother, Charlie. Labouring at
this impossible tree, they look like typical gyppo loggers. Except
this hopeful pair of Bamfield settlers is unusually prosperous:
they've bought 1,000 acres of this tough forest. They plan to cut
it down with this two-man saw, then farm it, a project that is in-
conceivable for man or devil, considering it takes two weeks to
remove *one* tree, to cut it down and burn the stump and roots out.
Yet these determined Swedes have laboured two years. But today
my dad puts down his end of the saw and says to Charlie: "No one
can ever cut this all down." It's the end of the mad plan.

Part of Bamfield in the 1930s. The shed at the far right is my father's; it sits on his
dock. Above it, with lettering on its roof, is the general store, and above that the post
office building. Uncle Charlie lived in the big house to its left; this was also the hotel.
The house with the covered porch just to the left of Uncle Charlie's place is my home.

A word from your museum guide:

That forest *has* been cut down today . . . modern power
saws. It's hard to know why Charlie didn't see that their
handsaw plan was hopeless, and see it much earlier. He'd

been a ship's carpenter. He should have known about trees and hard wood and saws and limitations. But he had a history of daring acts that had prospered. A few years before, he'd grown disenchanted as a ship's carpenter, jumped the ship in South Africa, worked in a mine there, lost an eye, made a mysterious bundle of money and then showed up in Canada. It had been his idea to buy the 1,000 acres, and he couldn't face defeat. So my dad had to be the one to say: Charlie, let's stop.

Village life

Gallery 1: Bamfield, 1950 — The morning bite

It is high summer in Bamfield, an hour before dawn, three o'clock in the morning. People are moving around outside (their flashlights show where they are). They are walking to The Creek. Maybe a quarter of the town are outside, women and men, the storekeeper, many aboriginals, a lot of the older children. Among the children is me, aged eight. Today it's my turn for the "morning bite." Some days I go, sometimes one of my sisters, sometimes my mother. Never my brother Henry — he's not in Bamfield anymore. Or my dad, because when he goes fishing, it's for weeks, in the big seiner, fishing in the inlets up and down the coast.

Most of the morning-bite boats are 15-foot clinkers — open boats with their wooden ribs showing inside, plank seats, a set of oars, and a small inboard engine that feeds on gasoline.

There's not much sound at this hour. No seagulls scream, the dogs haven't begun communicating, and the boats haven't started up. There's only the lap of the water at The Creek edge and a muffled scatter of human voices. But then the first boat engine starts, penetrating and as impossible to ignore as a dentist's drill. Other engines start, and it all begins to sound like a suburb of Vancouver with many people mowing their lawns at three o'clock in the morning. These boat engines *sound* like lawnmowers because that's about what they are — little gasoline engines near the centre of the boat, putting about six horsepower into a shaft to the propeller in the stern. (A few boats have this spinning shaft protected with a metal sleeve. Most just have the exposed shaft.)

A man helps me, because I'm too small to pull the starting rope. After the engine starts and settles in, I head out by myself.

Purple-black shapes of hills can be seen in the east. Out on The Creek, flashlights dart and flick. These small boats have no running lights. Some trollers, much larger boats with many lights, are heading out too. But they don't stay in The Creek.

Most of the natives are in dugouts, no bigger than the clinker boats — actual dug-out canoes, made from logs. Each is pushed along by a gasoline engine, the same as the clinker boats. Sort of lawnmower dugouts.

Your museum guide:

There are no outboard engines in 1950s Bamfield. They would have suited these little boats, but they came later. When they did, the natives used them too. With an outboard at full throttle, a native dugout went like a speedboat. And they were steered easily, just by leaning from side to side, the old way.

The Bamfield folk are on the dark water to catch salmon. The fish bite well this early, and the salmon get good prices from the scows in The Creek, which anchor there all summer. Once a week a big packer boat comes from Vancouver to collect the salmon all along the coast, and pour fresh ice into the scows.

It's started to rain lightly, a drizzle. Bamfield resembles a rain gauge. The great forest soaks up another slosh of daily rain, and the village experiences it and records it in their boat logs:

> 26 June, S.E. gale & rain
>
> 27 June, cold, rain
>
> 28 June, still raining
>
> 29 June, drizzle

By six o'clock in the morning, most fishing in The Creek stops. A couple of dozen salmon may lie in each boat, if it's been a good bite. Most of these fish are taken to the scows right away, exchanged for that Bamfield rarity — cash.

Your museum guide:

See what's different from fishing a few decades later? The morning-bite people *don't* fish 18 hours a day. They only put out a *few* hooks. They don't use seine nets, and they couldn't have imagined a powerful drag-net boat. The few large trollers in Bamfield — or my dad's seiner (the only one in the village) — might stay out a few weeks. But even those bigger boats didn't have slick navigation instruments, so they stayed close to shore. This style of fishing had gone on for decades in the village (and before that, for 5,000 years by the native population, up and down the coast). You see, there was no way this lightly equipped Bamfield fleet, numerous as they seemed, could harm the fishing stocks. Provided they kept away from the salmon-spawning places — and they did. Great numbers of salmon got past the fishing boats, even with the whole village's efforts peaking in the summer.

Bamfield in 1948, looking east across Bamfield Inlet to the Trans-Pacific Cable Station, left background. To its right is the *Princess Maquinna*, which brought freight

and passengers from Victoria every two weeks. The fishboats and dock in the fore-
ground belong to my father. The photograph was taken from our front porch.

Gallery 1: Bamfield, 1950 — The sea boon

Your museum guide:

First, a little more about *The Creek*. It's salt water, a long, lozenge-shaped inlet connected to the Pacific Ocean, maybe a half-mile across and five miles long. There is indeed a *creek* that feeds into it, Sugsaw Creek, an ample freshwater stream that some call the Sugsaw River. But in Bamfield, "The Creek" means the inlet.

Consider The Creek, as I am doing now at age eight — with a youthful pre-seafaring gaze, looking out the window at the gray inlet. From our house, it's only a minute's walk to the water. Right across The Creek stands the cable station, a building that looks like Alcatraz, and where Canada's phone calls head out undersea to other continents. Under that gray Creek surface are fish that never fail, fish that seem just as numerous and unstoppable as the rainforest trees that crowd Bamfield from the land side. To me, it seems a simple fact about all the fish, a richness that can be used to pay for this or that, at least in summer. And if winter turns hungry, the cash gone, the salmon away, then there are unfailing (but ugly-looking) ling cod. Not bad eating, and they can sometimes be sold — though not for much. Even children can't starve here among this watery richness, once they're old enough to dig clams. Some native boys have told me they *might* have starved without the clams — their parents could be away for days.

If by sorcery The Creek became still and transparent as glass — as I am imagining it by that window — there could be seen a gallery of life. The quick herring, the bright-tinted rockfish, the red snappers, the salmon, the flatfish, the small sharks (dogfish), sea lions and seals, and the summer schools of nearly whale-size basking sharks. And all the shell-fish: abalone, clams, oysters (no pearls in these oysters, just for eating) — and all still thriving.

Your museum guide:

Parts of the abalone beds could be seen without needing magically clear water. The abalone clustered in shallow water, as if they wanted company. At certain low tides, their shells were above the surface. But it was easy enough to find them at *any* low tide, by walking around in rubber boots. One abalone bed was at The Creek's edge below our house. So many abalone beds around, but only the storekeeper seemed to eat them. Most people ignored the abalone. What a difference in the 1970s! Abalone could suddenly be sold for $5 a pound to the Japanese. The Japanese transformed the market for abalone, and everything else.

Museum video: Bamfield, 1950 — The disappearing gillnet

Another summer day, raining again, and I crouch in the dim light of our net loft. Two boys are with me. We're considering the small gillnet stored there — it belongs to my dad. Maybe we'll use it to catch some herring. Then use the herring to bait salmon. We haven't done that before, using the gillnet. It lies bundled in the loft, forgotten. Should we? Shouldn't we? No one has said we *can't.*

In fifteen minutes, we're on The Creek in a clinker boat. Right away, the gillnet jams with herring, every mesh plugged, jerking. Herring! We've heard stories about great seine boats capsized by herring! Instead of 100 tons of herring in the seine net, suddenly there'd be 2,000 tons. Those 2,000 tons of live fish panic or collude, all swim *down* and their force flips the boat. But this morning the herring in our little gillnet just run off with the net — while we tug, tearing holes, and the net dives and vanishes, now the property of the fish.

Almost a year later, Dad wonders whatever happened to the gillnet. No one can remember.

Museum video: Bamfield, 1950 — The great fish

I cast a longline from the clinker boat and hook something. It's a slow fight to work the line in, with little jerks and accumulating successes. It seems to be a great fish like Santiago's in *The Old Man and the Sea*. A monster fish, as big as my boat! It thuds against the hull, knocking me sideways and shaking my confidence considerably. Unlike old Santiago, I cut this fish free. At home, they want to know about this fish. Maybe it was a huge skate? Or halibut? The great fish is a blur to me. Not enough clues. No one can identify it for sure.

Gallery 1: Bamfield, 1950 — Aboriginals

The Bamfield natives fish the same way as the whites, they dress like them, speak English, keep chickens and are equally poor. If there's any racism, I haven't sensed it. The aboriginals have the

Bamfield in 1932, looking west across the inlet from the cable station to Aguilar Point. The large float just left of centre is my father's; to its left on the shore sits his net shed. Just up the hill from that you can see the Wickham residence, and to its right Uncle Charlie's hotel. Right of that is the large post office building,

cheekbones and look of American Indians, but I have native friends and I have white friends. No matter about the style of cheekbones.

Your museum guide:

In 1876, the Canadian government asked the natives to point out where all their villages were. The government made those villages into reserve land, owned by the government but held for the natives. The land couldn't be sold. (The Canadian government took into account how American Indians had been given their reserve land outright, but had most often sold it, squandered the money, and lapsed into poverty.) What this bit of Canadian history means is that every good salmon stream or river in Canada has a native reserve at its entrance, because native villages were (sensibly) located there, in tribal days.

and the group of buildings on the water below it is the Coast Guard station. Off the right edge of the photo, Bamfield Inlet joins Trevor Channel, seen at the top of the picture, which forms part of Barkley Sound.

Photo courtesy of BC Archives, D-01364.

Gallery 1: Bamfield, 1950 — Lights

It is night, black. No streetlights, no moon. The only light is the glow from house windows. We have electric lights — but each house has to generate its own power. (The Canadian grid doesn't yet serve Bamfield.) A gasoline-powered generator, most often working in the woodshed and out of the weather, puts out DC power, like on a boat. It's enough wattage for lights and small loads, but not enough to run a fridge.

Your museum guide:

A few households had fridges that worked from bottled gas — a thermodynamic miracle, converting a gas flame into ice. I didn't see how it was possible. Our house got one when I was ten years old. It worked perfectly, with subdued gurgling sounds most of the time.

Gallery 1: Bamfield, 1950 — Shopping

There are no roads here so there's no road *out* of the town. To go anywhere — to Port Alberni, say — one travels by boat. To go further, like to Vancouver, Bamfield people might take a bus from Port Alberni. Or just go the whole way from Bamfield by boat.

With no cars, how do Bamfield people go *shopping*? The simple and natural way: they walk to the village store. Or pull their boat up there — it's right by a dock. If something is too heavy to carry back, they wheel it away in a hand-pulled wagon or wheelbarrow, or winch it into their boat.

The store sells groceries. Also fundamental hardware: things like buckets, glue, nails, brooms, string. There's no frozen food or chilled soft drinks. And no ice cream. Outside, by the dock, the store runs a marine gas station. Diesel can be bought, but in 1950 that's just coming in. Most people can't afford a diesel engine.

Bamfield doesn't depend completely on the store. The village is self-sufficient, if managing to live at a poverty level counts. People have garden plots. At the Wickhams', potatoes are a big crop (a favourite of Dad's). With a bit of cabbage and carrots and a few herbs, that's about it.

People with cows may barter milk for potatoes. Or natives spear crabs and exchange a few for apples. Other people trade directly through the store — walk in with a box of some surplus, and ring up credit that can be spent on nails, rubber boots, twine, candy.

Snapshots: Bamfield 1950

Your museum guide:

Let me pass around some photos, from the album in my head.

* That's me, with seven cod in a wooden-slat box. Caught in one morning. My family kept one, and I gave the rest to neighbours. Some things were given away like that. But the gifts returned, inevitably, in new forms. Not exactly barter. More like an overflow and circulation of excess.

* There's my dad, looking serious as usual, standing by an apple tree. There were plenty of apple trees on his land, but this tree was claimed by a native. A tradition. Way back, the native declared the tree was *his* and always had been. Dad didn't like this news, but shrugged. The native brought us crabs now and then, just gave them to us. Ownership was peculiar, blurred.

* There's another native, Denis, talking to Dad. Denis is average-sized, with bright eyes and an authoritarian voice. (Most natives tended to be withdrawing. Not Denis.) Dad is fixing an iron gate in his blacksmith shop. The story behind

this scene is involved. Denis has been hanging around, now and then praising Dad's boat, the *Cape May*. It wasn't being used much. (Dad came to prefer homesteading, not fishing.) Anyone witnessing the scene might detect that Denis is after something, but things in Bamfield are a little indirect, offhand. A certain measure of wheedling by Denis had been going on for weeks. He sat around and yakked, and helped, casually, and kept praising the boat. Such a wonderful boat, Denis said, there's no way someone like himself could possibly run it — though he *is* a skilled fisherman, very responsible, with great experience. He never came out and said: "Hey, I'd like to run your boat this year." This would mean he'd split the catch with my dad in a standard Bamfield way. No need to negotiate. All very simple, because if you ran someone's boat, everyone knew what the boat share was and what the crew share was. Today, in this photo, my Dad looked up, gazed at Denis for about two seconds, and *offered* to let him run the boat. Dad just gave in suddenly, like an overloaded camel. Even so, Denis didn't say, "Sure! Right!" Instead, he kept playing with a fishing weight in his hand, "Well, I'm not sure if I can handle the responsibility, but I sure would like to try." Which meant the deal was done. As indirectly as possible.

* Twice a week the freight boat from Port Alberni comes in. The shopkeeper's crates are winched out of the boat and onto the dock, and a crowd collects. They also ordered stuff — from catalogues — and their orders are on the boat.

* That's me from the back, carrying a metal container. I picked it up from a stump, right at the edge of the forest. A neighbour had left it there, a halfway pickup point between our houses.

The silvery container holds milk and has handles like ears. As I walk along (at a slight slant), I look out for cougars (though no one has seen the animals in daylight here). For years, I pick up the milk. The cougars, if there are any, just watch.

* There's a gang of fishermen hanging out at Ostroms — the only machine shop in Bamfield. Ostroms has been there eternally, it seems. Fishermen could get coffee, sit around and talk about how the world was rotting away. In a haul-out section by the dock, men worked on their boats. It didn't cost anything to use the haul-out for painting and small jobs. But to use the machine shop, there was a fee.

* My dad is adding a room to the house. That's the framework there. *Some* progress at least. For tricky bits, like built-in cupboards, he'll do a barter deal with a carpenter — not Charlie, because he is in hospital with a stroke. There is no "builder" in town. Everyone builds their own houses, extends them, fixes them — with some help.

* My mother stands at the stove. Potatoes are boiling in that iron pot — there are *always* potatoes for dinner. And usually boiled fish. Sometimes beef or ham, from the freight boat. Not much beef or pork comes from Bamfield itself. With the rainforest pressing up against the village, there is too little grazing land. Between meals, we Wickham kids sometimes spread peanut butter on the abominable white bread from the store. Once a week or so, Mum bakes her own bread. A treat.

* Three men sit by the dock, looking spaced out. It's winter, there's no fishing, not much to do, and they've found enough money to get drunk. There is no Bamfield Temperance Society

to help them, but the village has a built-in temperance system: it's hard to *afford* to get drunk. They mainly drink beer because of the price, but would drink anything they had the money for. The law said natives couldn't have alcohol at all, but they bought it from white friends.

* That's me there, in the chicken run. I've just counted 62 of the wary birds. (They sense I'm up to something.) A few chickens are sometimes taken by wild minks, so I keep a tally. And it's my job to keep them boarded up at night. The Wickhams had *always* had chickens. I'd heard stories about when we had hundreds. Enthusiasm ran high in the old times. Now there were only enough for eggs and the occasional chicken dinner. And in a few minutes, there would be 61 chickens. My sister Anne would have the job of plucking. Her turn.

* That's our garden. You see no fenced-in animals, anywhere in view from our house. No goats and pigs. No animals at all. Our neighbours keep a few goats, but pigs are rare in Bamfield. The Wickhams gave up on goats and pigs years ago, because of cougars. Even in 1950, cougars still killed some dogs. Imagine it's night, quiet, four kids are in the living room, playing cards. Then they stop. There's a snapping and squealing from the open storage place under the house. It's where the mother dog and her pups are. The kids don't dare to look, but they know the dogs are all dead. And they are.

* That's Charlie and my dad, in the early years, in that skiff, right out in the ocean. Yes, that's a cow with them, looking concerned, trying to keep her balance. They are *rowing* this bulky animal to Port Alberni, to get her mated. But the cow grows more and more unhappy. The boat lurches, the animal

Bamfield fisherfolk.

is suddenly overboard, swimming for land. When she gets her hooves on land, she disappears into the forest. Charlie and my dad exchange looks. That's it! No more cows, the hell with it!

Gallery 1: Bamfield, 1950 — Charlie's money

Charlie had money, probably in cash, and a pile of it. Like $crooge McDuck. Then Charlie suffered a stroke. For the rest of his life — years — he was bedridden, nearly paralyzed, in the hospital on Salt Spring Island (a day's boat trip from Bamfield).

How was this medical calamity to be paid for? Dad found cash in Charlie's house — quite a bit — and used that to pay Charlie's first hospital bills. But it still didn't add up: that couldn't have been *all* of Charlie's money. Dad lifted floor boards, poked bent wire into wall cavities, got discouraged, then tried again. The hunt went on for a year. But no more money was found. So Dad started to pay part of the hospital bills himself, with the government paying the rest.

Meanwhile, Charlie couldn't speak or write. His mind seemed remote. And there's me as a boy, sitting by the hospital bed on one of the Wickham family's visits. Charlie lies quietly, his face nearly blank, his glass eye adding to his blank look. All at once, he appears to recognize his visitors. He starts thrashing around, looking wild, as if trying to communicate something. It occurs to me that Charlie is trying to say where the money is! But no message comes forth. Then or ever.

Gallery 1: Bamfield, 1950 — Law and order

There are no locks on the houses in Bamfield. Theft would be like a theft in the family. How could the stolen thing be used, with everyone there to see?

With so little cash, no locks, such a small place, can it be there's no trouble? Not quite. There are numerous subdued squab-bles, like gusts of wind. Plus several feuds that blow like hard trade winds. The causes of trouble, large and small, are the same age-old causes that festered in stone-age caves or Tudor castles, and now fester in Bamfield. To mention one: a certain amount of sleeping around happens, which can bring pretty hot problems. But the heat is quenched, and somehow without murder.

See those two powerfully-built men, walking toward each other along the water's edge? They're beginning to behave like magnetic poles that repel. They've changed direction a little, they're avoid-ing each other, they aren't even looking or glancing at the other. Trouble is being avoided. That's most often what happens.

No police live in Bamfield, but their boat cruises the whole west Vancouver Island coast. Every couple of months, it docks in Bamfield. No mayor or government representative comes down to greet it. Such people don't exist. Instead, the police go to the store and have a coffee. If somebody in Bamfield has a problem, they can have a quiet word. It's how the coastal patrol works. From coffee to coffee.

Gallery 1: Bamfield, 1950 — The telephone

There's exactly one telephone in 1950s Bamfield. It's in a red phone box outside the village store. That phone is ringing now. It's a dull-black thing, heavy, made of brittle-looking plastic, equipped with a crank handle. And it's a rare thing for it to ring, because phone calls are steeply priced. Worse, they always mean emergency or death. The storekeeper, a wiry, high-energy man, bounds out of the store and lifts the black instrument. A correctly alarmed look forms on his face. He then springs and scurries the hundred yards up the trail to the Wickhams' house.

"Henry called!" he yells through the screen door. A few faces gather. "Call Henry, right away!" the storekeeper tells them. My dad puts down his pipe and does a long-legged canter down the trail to the phone. He receives heavy news, none heavier: Charlie has died.

This grim phone connects through a ramshackle, much-mended wire that runs miles through forest to Port Alberni. From there, it connects to the wider world of wires and phone talk. A Bamfield man named Burkholder has the full-time mission of keeping this line open, working against the gods of forest and tempest and snowfall — whose spiteful purpose is to snap the line in places that are hard to find.

B.C. Tel pays Burkholder a wage, and supplies a reliable boat. From the boat, Burkholder can see the phone line, most of it, hanging like a vine from tree to tree, close along the shore usually. Sometimes he has to land a little skiff on whatever gravel inlet he can find, walk and push through undergrowth, and carry out technical tests with a meter.

This phone system at least has the charm of technical simplicity: anyone in Bamfield can understand roughly how it works. It's only one step up from tin cans and a string. Later, a few families in Bamfield get crank phones installed in their own homes. To phone someone, they use a code: two quick cranks for the Burkholders, three for the Ostroms, one long and two shorts for the Fullertons — that sort of system. (There's no code for the phoneless Wickhams.) To phone out of Bamfield, it was necessary to get virtuoso help from an operator in Port Alberni.

Gallery 1: Bamfield, 1950 — The health-care system

The Red Cross Society runs Bamfield's "outpost hospital." It's more like a day-care centre, with a rotation of resident nurses. The nurse can remedy many illnesses or accidents . . . like me there, with a hook in my hand. The nurse cuts it out, then stitches. It's the only time I've been a patient here, or that I'll ever need to be (as life turned out).

For cases with greater peril or gore, or deeper medical mystery, the emergency float-plane can be called. It lands in Bamfield Creek, then flies the victim to Port Alberni, usually. But this private aircraft has to be paid for. So it *isn't* called in most cases. More often, the injured person is taken away by boat — even by dugout, if the victim is a native.

If a patient defies the Red Cross and *dies* in Bamfield, then the deceased still isn't *buried* in Bamfield. He or she is conveyed to Port Alberni and buried there. I can never find out why. Maybe no one knows. Anyway, few people do *die* here — because critical cases are sent to Port Alberni while they're still breathing. If they don't pull through, their last hour is usually in a hospital there. And they're buried in Port Alberni.

The Wickhams' next-door neighbour happens to be a retired nurse. I hang around there sometimes. I'm there now, when a native woman knocks. She's pregnant and I listen to her ask the old nurse for advice about a home birth. (She has come here because the Red Cross nurse isn't in town right now.) The old nurse shakes her head. The native woman has had too many complications in her births before. She'll have to have her baby in the Port Alberni hospital. Two weeks later, I see the woman and her husband get into a dugout canoe, and head out.

Gallery 1: Bamfield, 1950 — The outside world

Your museum guide:

These 300 Bamfield souls, this timeless village with its eternal fisherfolk, may seem quaint, or maybe enviable. But *they* imagined that real life happened in a world outside. They found out what they could about that world, and sometimes dreamed of joining it. To them, their own lives seemed nothing special. Some hated Bamfield, and felt like captives.

There's me, outside the storekeeper's house, with a bunch of other boys. We're sitting or slouching on a bench, and stare through a window at a TV. A loudspeaker is rigged up outside, so we can hear. (The storekeeper doesn't want us in his living room.) The primitive black-and-white TV stays on all day, with a window full of eyes outside.

We learn what we can from Roy Rogers, Lassie, Howdy Doody, Dragnet, Red Skelton, and I Love Lucy. The world out there that we *haven't* seen is so wide and bright.

Your museum guide:

When my mother was old, I realized she'd lived her life mostly *through* people who came to our house and told us about the world. It was common to sit around and tell stories. And listen closely. Mum never went anywhere.

Here's a native boy who's told me that he wants to become a *doctor*. That's as amazing as if he announced he was planning to become Superman. I can't take it in. I've never *seen* a doctor. They're from an exterior planet. How could a boy from Bamfield become a doctor? Boys here go into fishing.

Your museum guide:

One of my Bamfield friends went to university, and became a city lumber broker. Going to university seemed so foreign, so unlikely to us. Just to get out of Bamfield to continue *high school* was an accomplishment.

Gallery 2: Bamfield, 1908 — Taxes and licences

When Charlie came to Bamfield in 1908, there was one universal Canadian tax: a "head tax": $5 a year. But most Bamfield people were exempt — fishermen, farmers, and natives.

Gallery 1: Bamfield, 1950 — Taxes and licences

I never hear any grumbles about income tax. If the tax exists, everyone in Bamfield is too low on the scale to pay anything.

There's an annual land tax. Everyone with property in Bamfield gets hit with that once a year. And anyone who wants to fish needs a licence. Which is almost everyone. It's $5 a year, no matter if it's for the morning bite, or to run a troller and stay out for weeks. Catch as much as you like, all year, for $5! How's that for a fishing licence?

Your museum guide:

I hired an accountant in Vancouver, in my late twenties. He specialized in the fishing business. He said that Bamfield fishermen started paying income tax in the mid-1960s. This makes sense — that's when the Japanese market for Canadian fish started to kick in and the prices went up. We could make money, not just survive.

There's one limit on the fishing licence: no fishing up the rivers in places where the salmon spawn — too destructive. Every river has a white sign, six feet high, to mark that boundary. Any higher upriver than that, and it's NO FISHING. That's enforced by a watchful village, not by patrol boats. (The patrol boat comes too rarely. But if any outrageous poaching goes on, the patrol boat will be told about it when they show up.)

Consider me and those two boys, with a clinker boat anchored in the Sugsaw River. It's summer, we're in the water, splashing, messing around. Chum salmon hang out here, and we chase the fish, grab their tails, pretend to fight with them. Three weeks later when the patrol boat comes in, guess what? The patrol officer comes to the Wickhams' house for a cup of coffee. This has happened before, but rarely. Something is up. The officer gets around to mentioning that some kids were bothering the salmon upriver, and those kids should damn well smarten up or they'll be in trouble. The message is understood.

There's a native village by that river where the boys chased the salmon (wonder how the patrol boat found out?). The village lies a mile inside the no-fishing boundary. The natives might fish there a little, illegally, for food fish. But for their commercial fishing, they always go *outside* the boundary and fish with the rest of Bamfield. Like those aboriginal boats coming down the Sugsaw now, passing above thousands of chum in the no-fishing area, then joining the rest of the Bamfield fishing boats — where there are *no* fish.

Gallery 1: Bamfield, 1950 — School

This is the Bamfield school. That's right: only three rooms. One stressed-out teacher per room, who drills and possibly inspires combined classes of different ages (grades one to three in one class, for example). Everyone goes to this school: natives, poor whites, and the well-off cable-station kids. Up to the age of 14. After that, the closest high school is in Port Alberni — too far to run back and forth by boat. To go to high school means living with relatives there. Few get there.

Your museum guide:

I nearly flunked grade one. In grade five, we were given an aptitude test. The teacher broke the news to me: I was too dumb to ever go to the university. This didn't disturb me much. (University! Heh.) When I was 14, I went to live with my sister Karen and her husband in Fort Knox, Kentucky (where the gold is stored). The town seemed so strange that I withdrew my feelers and was suddenly shy. I even fell into studiousness. Out of that cocoon, I emerged as a straight-A student. I left Fort Knox after three years, carrying some of that knowledge like useful gold coins. The school secretary also handed me my records to take back to Canada. Why she trusted me to carry this stuff, I don't know. Reading it, as the train rolled north, I saw I had a respectably high IQ. According to that, I was at least smart enough to make a difference, whether I ran a fishing boat or a business.

Gallery 1: Bamfield, 1950 — Slaughter of the basking sharks

Basking sharks are the second-largest fish in the world (one size smaller than the whale shark). Their cavernous mouths filter the sea-water for plankton, baby fish, and fish eggs. On this unlikely diet they manage to grow to 35 feet and four tons. These beasts move slowly, about 3 mph top speed, and they're harmless to people. (The reverse isn't true.) Here in 1950s Bamfield, they're plentiful.

Because the basking sharks are harmless, but gigantic, they invite pranks. Boys in boats sometimes ram them. It's like running into a soft rock. Hey! Then watch the great, mildly annoyed fish get the message and slowly dive.

The pranks get rougher. I pull alongside one of the inoffensive fish, and jam a spear into it. I'd made the spear: a sharp metal shaft, fixed to a pole at a single pivot. A cord on the pole is used to turn the spear-point sideways inside the fish, and lock it there. The stricken creature dives in slow motion as I play out line, like a whaler (which I imagine I am). I get towed for a mile by the dying creature. After that, I tow *it*, now a dead weight truly. At the dock by the village store, where people cluster, the young whaler hooks the fish up to a cargo winch and hauls it partway out of the water. To show it off.

Now observe grown men at their pranks. A DFO patrol boat

— symbolic protector of fish — but with its bow made into a *knife*. The whole leading edge of the boat, the part under water, has been fitted with a knife-edge. The boat cuts the water well, with this blade slicing ahead. And cuts anything else it hits. Like the basking sharks the boat deliberately rams. Some of the great fish are cut in two. Some are gashed and die thrashing.

In the Summer of the Basking Shark Deaths, I count 63 dead. Then see no more of the fish that summer. The DFO has killed them all. The fish — and their parts — float ashore in Barkley Sound, outside The Creek. The smell is stomach-turning.

No one in Bamfield quite understands why this slaughter happens. When it's talked over, they think that the DFO men did it for sport. Because they were bored. No better explanation is ever offered. (The official DFO explanation, years later, was that the basking sharks were a menace to gillnets and were culled for that reason. But gillnets were rarely used in those days.)

Your museum guide:

This slaughter *was* outrageous, but there was a killing culture then. If you carried a gun, and some wild animal was moving, it was a casual target. Nobody thought about it. The DFO guys cruised around that inlet in the summer, there wasn't a hell of a lot to do, so they attacked basking sharks. It didn't dawn on anyone that the sharks were a local population, like salmon, that came to this particular inlet. Next year, none showed up. People noticed they were missing, but thought they'd gone somewhere else that season. Years went by, and the fish never came back. They're now rare everywhere in British Columbia. The attitude then was that fish were unlimited, impossible to damage. Even DFO officials thought so.

Bamfield today

Today there's no morning bite in Bamfield. The old village was all about salmon, and they are gone. There are no small fishing boats, no big seiners, no commercial fishing left at all.

None of my family live in Bamfield. None of their offspring live there. The Bamfield where I grew up is a holiday place. It has web sites devoted to it, praising it for its scenery, peace — yes, and fishing (find them if you can). There's a road out now, 95 kilometres of gravel logging road. And there's "float-plane service available from Vancouver, Nanaimo, Victoria and Port Alberni. Check with your airline or travel agent for details."

Earlier I talked about the general salmon decline in British Columbia. And here we have this little village, a kind of microscope that might be used to focus very finely and try to see exactly what caused the decline (the topic of the next chapter). If we can see it clearly for Bamfield, the same applies to those hundreds of villages along the coast. They aren't salmon villages anymore. That's history. Something for a museum.

6

The scholar's plan

"Davis Plan?" I asked Henry. There'd been some radio talk among the boat crews.

Henry stared at the horizon, like he was looking for a cloud the size of a man's hand. We were 125 miles off Alaska, the sky was broad and clear, and we were hunting halibut. "If you've got a boat, you get a licence. It's nothing."

It was 1968. Jack Davis, former Rhodes scholar, was now federal Minister of Fisheries. With such credentials, how could the nation go wrong? It was his boat-licensing plan that had just come in. He insisted the salmon-fishing fleet was too big, so he was going to stop it from getting bigger. That was step one. Everyone who had a boat automatically got a licence, and it didn't cost much. No one *else* got a licence, unless they could buy one from someone who was willing to sell theirs.

"Right, no extra competitors!" I announced to Henry. "That's good." Now I've made some faulty statements in my life, but this one was like the soldier who said, "Don't sweat it. Rifle fire can never hit us at this dist-"

The ominous part of the Davis Plan never worried me: if someone bought two or more boat licences (or owned them already), they could combine the licences into a single licence — for a boat as long as the single licences put together. See? Buy two licences for native canoes, each 20 feet long, then convert that to a licence for a single boat that's 40 feet long.

So what? That's what we all thought. This simple 20 + 20 = 40 arithmetic blocked critical thought. It took time for the logical consequences to crunch all the little salmon boats in BC.

I didn't live in Bamfield in the years after the Davis Plan. Mostly I was out on the tossing sea, crewing for people. Way out there. First on Henry's seiner and long-liner. Then on other serious boats. When I went to Bamfield, it was brief, which gave me a time-lapse impression of the place — a bit like those movies of daisies closing at great speed, because the frames were taken at ten-minute intervals but replayed at normal movie pace. When my brain put my personal Bamfield frames together, I was startled at what was happening.

I was told that one man had retired and sold his salmon licence for a few hundred dollars to an outsider. On my next trip, I heard that someone had had a bad year, heavy financial problems, and had sold their boat licence for what amounted to a year's catch. Little by little, the Bamfield fleet was contracting, like a shrinking run of salmon.

Remember Denis? I found him building a boat, up on the beach in front of his house. His old father was helping and whistling. The boat was going to be a beauty, a 35-footer. Denis got the licence by taking a licence he had for a smaller boat and adding a canoe licence he'd bought. Seven months later, I saw him again. The fine boat was finished. Denis took me out, telling me about it in a voice as proud as the sea wind. One year later, he'd sold the boat and the licence. He was out of fishing for good. He did it because he'd owed money building the boat, the season had been terrible, but by then the licence had risen in value. So the licence had become just another thing to sell.

Hold on. The licence had risen in value? Now why was that, Sherlock? Because someone wanted to *buy* licences. Certain big companies, for example. A licence gave a right to fish, with no limit on the catch. The catch only depended on skill, some luck, and the technical powers that were loaded into the boat. A licence was for a certain *length* of boat. Nothing else. A boat of almost supernatural power, a 45-foot seiner, one that cost $1 million to build, ran with a crew of eight and had a 600-yard net, was considered by the DFO as equal to three primitive 15-foot dugouts, each with one man and one line overboard. Uh-huh.

In 1968, salmon licences cost about $10 per foot of boat. By the time I bought *Joy II*, licences were still fairly cheap — the licence for that first boat cost me about $400 out of the total $7,000 price. Ten years later, the licence for the same *length* of boat (any 32-foot boat) could be sold for $75,000!

Meanwhile licences began to fall on other kinds of fishermen, not just salmon fishermen. As soon as the DFO realized a fish was valuable, they licensed it. Consider the case of Barry McFadden. He fished for geoducks, when he wasn't crewing for me. He actually started the geoduck business, by finding and gathering them (a kind of clam, remember), loading them in the back of his pickup, and selling them in Vancouver's Chinatown alleys. The Chinese sampled the clams and liked them. Barry only got four cents a pound, but it was something to sell in the salmon off-season.

The Chinese appreciation for geoducks gradually advanced to Hong Kong and the Chinese diaspora. Note that Barry didn't need a licence to start this. The DFO probably didn't know that geoducks existed. Barry — and then a couple of other guys — built the enterprise without one government dollar. But when the geoduck price started going up, the DFO's mind snapped open like a hungry clam and decided to "regulate" things. But they didn't *help* in any way.

Barry was issued a geoduck licence, because he was already doing it. (Same idea as for salmon licences.) Two years later, he sold that licence for $40,000. He thought it was a huge sum. For the next ten years, he worked for me as a deck hand. But every year his face fell a bit more, as the geoduck licences rose in value. On his last trip with me, the licence he'd sold for $40,000 had bloated to $400,000. Then it went to $1.5 million! Barry, who started the business, was never able to get back in.

Such was the pattern. Little boats were selling out. This went on until Bamfield had *no* little boats left. That took about 15 years. Even Bamfield's commercial seiners and trollers left the village. Instead of a Bamfield troller delivering its catch into a packer boat anchored in Bamfield Creek, the catch had to be taken straight to Vancouver. That's how the corporations wanted it. Big boats, even ones still run by Bamfield people, only ducked into Bamfield during rough weather, or to say hello.

Natives were victims too, all up and down the BC coast. Here's Modestus Nobels, pleading for native communities near Prince Rupert: "We've watched our fleet in the north drift away from us, slowly, piece by piece, as changes to the management of the fishery have come about. Economic stresses have driven people out of the area, either to sell their licences or to move on to other opportunities. . . . We are a fishing community. The reality is that we have nothing else. This is what we want. This is not a job. This is a life. It is a culture, one that is being systematically destroyed, destroyed in some proportion by greed and in others by pure stupidity. . . . I speak for a group of people who are so demoralized at this point that they have a hard time even speaking for themselves."

The number of big seiners almost doubled, while little boats were hauled up on land and began to rot. The big seiners *didn't* sell their licences to the government and have them cancelled. No way. Only the owners of little boats cashed in to the DFO.

You may wonder: why did *anyone* sell their licences in these government "buy-backs"? Didn't they know that commercial buyers were out there all the time — powerful companies that would snap up a boat licence of any length? Some did, but the government offers were OK. And no one rang a bell and explained what was happening. It was smart for the big groups to buy quietly, without bidding up the costs of licences too much. If they had to watch a scattering of fishermen sell to the government buy-backs, well that was bearable.

A few lucky Bamfield fishermen *started* with big boats, or managed to get one soon enough, then held on. They did OK. The rest of Bamfield was slowly exiled from fishing.

I took over my dad's boat fairly early in all this, the 45-foot *Cape May*. It grew valuable. It would have gotten *more* valuable if I hadn't been penny-pinching. The *Cape May* came with a seine licence, but that cost more to renew than a troller licence, so I downgraded to a troller licence. I was probably the only one who ever did that.

Meanwhile Bamfield adjusted to its spreading deprivation like it was some extended worsening of the weather. Fishermen are *used* to accepting things, while remaining packed with hope. After all, fish seem to come from nowhere, sometimes disappear back to nowhere for a few seasons, then mysteriously come back. Hey, something will turn up! But for most Bamfield people, nothing ever did.

Politicians still congratulate themselves. "When I first served in Parliament," recalls David Anderson, "from 1968 to 1972, I was elected a member of the Fisheries Committee. That was the first time — that I can recollect — we had a fleet-reduction program in British Columbia. There may have been a previous one, but that's the first one I recollect. It was called the Davis Plan. And it worked."

Fleet reduction? Why reduce the fleet, but do it in a way that multiplies the fishing power? In my most charitable mood, I

might say that our honourable representatives started out thinking that the *number* of boats was all that mattered. They may
have been sincere about that. Cut the numbers by half, and you
cut the catch by half . . . maybe? But in their legislative planning, they soon saw there was more to it — so threw in that part
about boat length, before they announced the licensing. As if
fishing boats were identical but came in different lengths, like
sections of pipe.

But how could they go on believing this was working? They
ran the licensing. They couldn't possibly *not* notice what was
happening, the gathering of the licences into fewer and fewer
hands, the big companies taking over, and the increasing power
of their boats.

Here's my hard judgment: Ottawa has always hungered to turn
fishing over to the big companies, because it simplifies their regulation of the industry. They only have to deal with a few fishing-
company executives, who share a lot of their views about the
world and have a certain style of life. No rough fishermen walk
in, wearing torn clothes and smelling of fish. Even back in the
1880s, Ottawa tried to limit the fishing licences on the Fraser,
supposedly because of worries about declining runs. (Notice the
pattern: something's gone wrong, so we'll take over!) They gave
up on that in 1892, but they *didn't* stop Eastern banks from financ-
ing a monopoly takeover of the canneries.

In WW II, about 1,200 Japanese fishing boats were seized by
the government. Many were owned by Japanese Canadians. The
government later sold the boats at knockdown prices to . . . yep,
the packing companies.

In the heavy years since the Davis Plan, there've been more
"reforms," and endless patched-on amendments and improve-
ments. Licences have been put on anything that lives under water,
including red and green sea urchins (I'm not making that up).

Any independent fishermen who manage to survive have to keep adjusting to the practical aim of catching as many fish as they can, allowing for the latest round of baffling and possibly insane rules. What else are they supposed to do?

The DFO *must* have noticed that fishermen and fishing companies had mighty impulses to catch fish. Because the DFO next flapped around and started restricting the length of boats and anything else that came to mind. But even that never stopped the fishermen. They'd find a way, if there was one, to get one up on the other fishermen. Their licences said they could fish, and those fish belonged to *them* — once they were caught.

It's an age-old idea that fish in the sea belong to everyone, until they're caught. It goes back to Roman law. No one could claim fish were their property until they *landed* the fish. Which was no problem, as long as there were enough fish. As I've said about 20 times in this book, fishermen used to think the fish were inexhaustible. There was no "scarcity." Therefore no pressure to work out who had the rights to the fish. Every boat owner had every motive to expand his fishing power. Fleets expanded, their costs kept rising, their technology kept advancing, and it ended in a bureaucratic and corporate bog: over-capacity, ruinously expensive boats, low fishing stocks, poor catches, and near-zero profits.

Before the Davis Plan, *everybody* in BC had a right to fish. After it, anyone *without* a licence was out. It was the end of the old Roman law. But the plan backfired because of the fishing power of the big boats. So the DFO kept panicking or plotting, and "protected stocks" by cutting seasons and putting so many restrictions on boats they were hardly allowed to get wet. Some herring seasons were cut to as little as 15 minutes a year. In case you missed that: *15 minutes a year.* Another example: the seine fleet fished 24 days in the Upper Johnstone Strait in 1982, but was cut to three days by 1994. Anxious people feared that if a proposed fourth day hadn't been stopped, the fleet would have wiped out the stock.

Meanwhile there were backwaters of sanity: halibut and black-cod fishermen had agreed on their own fishing quotas. They did that by brooding and arguing about how to divide the total allowed catch. For black cod, a fisherman's quota was based on his catch in the last three years. From then on, each fisherman was allowed that exact percentage of the total catch. And the total catch was set by the DFO, using a lot of research about the fish stocks.

The black-cod fishermen pay for the research. They obviously *want* to know what's happening, and don't want to hurt the stocks in a situation like this.

Fishermen often *fight* a quota system at first. Because they're used to struggling for their share of the catch, grabbing someone else's share if they can. Quotas spoil this adrenaline rush. But fishermen who join a quota system begin to feel like joint owners of the fish stocks. And that changes everything. As I'm about to tell you.

7

When the fishermen take over

In 1983 I bought a new boat, the *Nordic Spirit*, a 48-footer, filled with the sort of spirit I needed — Viking get-up-and-go. I was feeling the weight of the global economic slump. World fish prices were way down, the salmon season was down to a bare three months, but my monthly boat payments stayed fixed and high. How could Eric Wickham, son of Norsemen, hope to prosper in these circumstances?

Maybe by catching other fish in the nine months when we weren't allowed to catch salmon? It couldn't be halibut, because the off-season was almost the same as salmon's. Which left . . . what? Only a few strange fish that no one cared about.

Yet I had a bright thought. There were black cod out there all the time. I always caught a few when I was long-lining for halibut. Black cod were viewed as junk, and I'd only used them as halibut bait. But they could also be sold, for a low price. I had no idea *why* there was a market at all, because I'd never met anyone who ate these fish.

Let me tell you that black cod aren't really cod. They're more properly called "sablefish" (*Anoplopoma fimbria*). They're sleek fish, with black skin and they live in the cold, deep waters of the North Pacific. They weigh about as much as salmon.

As I was thinking about these fish, and the nine months ahead with no salmon, I was struck by other curious matters and portents.

Like this one: a man named Blair Pearl had been out there catching black cod with his big boat. Why? I knew he fished a long way from shore and used traps set in deep water. He seemed to get a good weight of fish. There were also a couple of guys with smaller boats who'd been trying to long-line black cod, instead of using traps. But they didn't seem to get much. Anyway, something was up. What was I missing? I'd been fishing only salmon and halibut.

With energy that can sometimes pour into a troubled man, I refitted the *Nordic Spirit* to chase black cod — to join that little mystery fleet and see what was going on.

First I needed black-cod traps. Let me tell you how I got them. As it happened, two guys who'd been crew members on Blair's black-cod boat had actually *built* the *Nordic Spirit* — the new boat I'd bought. Those two guys must have been inspired by what they'd seen out there on Blair's boat, because they'd decided to go into black-cod fishing themselves. (Another powerful signal: something was up with those black cod.) Their boat was launched about the time the hard economic winds began to blow in 1981. They couldn't meet their payments, and the bank took their boat. (I bought it from the bank, in fact.) But the woeful two told me they'd kept their black-cod traps. There was no mortgage on those, so they'd stored them in a basement. (Fishermen are like that: if something is useless, store it.) I paid them a visit, swapped a few grim jokes, made an offer and went off with all their traps, upsetting the hairy brown spiders in their basement. Two hundred standard traps, looking new enough to have come right from the manufacturer.

It needed many trips to collect them in my pickup, because these traps aren't small. They're shaped like giant lampshades (circular top and bottom, and tapered sides) and stand waist-high. All the sides are covered with plastic-rope netting, stretched tight over a metal frame. In one side, there's a little tunnel of net that ends in the middle of the trap, with a flap at the end. The fish smell the bait in the trap, swim down the tunnel, push the flap to get in, but can't work out how to get back out. (The gods trap men in similar ways, and this chapter has examples.)

I coiled several miles of plastic rope into the *Nordic Spirit*'s fish-hold. A big fish-hold, it could store 20 tons of frozen fish. I needed that much rope, because I planned to put out several lines, with 50 traps on each. I also had to allow 3,000 feet of line rising from the bottom at each end. You can see I had this all worked out. I *thought* I had it all worked out.

Everything was ready. The miles of rope in the fish-hold, traps stacked everywhere, and a bold crew of four. But with my fish-hold choked with rope, where did I mean to store the catch? Basic! In this type of fishing, the traps are left in the water for the whole season. Every few days you lift a line of traps, take out the fish and lower the traps again, then proceed to shore with each new catch. In my calculations, my cheerful theoretical work, it was clear that hauling up one line with 50 traps wouldn't jam the decks with too many traps and too much line. We'd still have space to clean the fish, put them in the freezer (now empty of rope), put the traps back down — and head for shore, heavy in the water with our tons of black cod.

The guys who sold me the traps said that if they were left down there too long, the fish would eat each other and I could end up with one overfed black cod in each trap. The fish were safe to leave in the traps for about six days. It was the first time I'd had any reliable info. Or *maybe* reliable info. These were bankrupt fishermen.

It pleased me to see how neatly it was possible to stack the traps, considering the number I had. The circular net peels off the bottom of the trap by releasing a line. That line also releases a second line that holds up the little tunnel I've mentioned. The tunnel sags and you can stack one conical trap inside the other.

At this stage, most of the deck space was taken up with stacks of traps, which resembled giant termite mounds. We had to walk on top of them in some places — they were strong enough. Traps even blocked the galley door. To get grub or coffee, we worked our way to the bow, groped through the pilot-house door, and then spelunked back like subterranean explorers through tight passages and got to the galley that way.

In case you're wondering: didn't the two guys who built the boat have the same trouble with all this clutter? They did! The common mania is to take out as many traps as you can, because once they're in the water, you're OK. And you get maximum fishing power that way.

With this heavy weight of gear but light knowledge, I travelled up the West Coast of Vancouver Island, then stopped about 40 miles off. *My* waters. I knew the place. It gave me a good feeling, even if it was February and temperatures were just above freezing. I didn't get ice in my hair, like Admiral Byrd at the South Pole, but now and then there'd be light hail and wildly whirling snowflakes. The wind was blowing more than 20 knots. The boat jumped and rolled, and I warily contemplated setting out the traps. A 20-knot wind was about the limit of feasible fishing with these traps, as I immediately found out. The wind caught the big lamp-shades and made them seem like living creatures. They wanted to twist out of our hands, leap overboard and join the sea life.

I guess that the *Nordic Spirit* was one of five boats out there that February. If more boats had been doing anything as peculiar in February as trying to catch black cod, I would have heard about it. Definitely. Everybody (including me) was still making some money on salmon. That was fished in summer, in balmy weather, working the inlets. We did it wearing golfing clothes.

So comfortable compared to me now, wearing my Admiral Byrd outfit and scowling face.

We struggled. We slid around the windy deck. And at last we managed to put the traps out. They each clipped onto a line, the way I clipped on hooks when I had *Joy II*. At each end of the line, we fastened three fluoro-red buoys, the size of giant beach balls or balloons, creating a kind of party atmosphere. I used three buoys, because there had to be enough flotation to hold up 3,000 feet of line that descended to the depths (black cod lurk deep). Each cluster of buoys was fixed with an anchor — a 50-pound one, shaped like anchors usually are. (This turned out to be a bad idea, because their barb-like ends sometimes snagged 3,000 feet down. Later, I'd use shapeless and snag-free 200-pound hunks of steel for anchors.)

As soon as all the traps were out (four lines of them, 50 traps on each), I grew edgy. The first line of traps had already been in the water six hours. Plenty of time to get packed with black cod! I took the boat back to that first line, and hesitated. I paced back and forth in a tight section of deck, in the manner of Julius Caesar deciding whether to cross the Rubicon Stream. Overwhelmed with strong intuitions, I suddenly ordered the crew: "Bring them in! Let's see what we've got!"

The crew brought up the anchor, and started to winch in the line of traps. The winch gave a pinched squeal, the sound a man struck with a sudden hernia might have made. The line to the traps didn't budge. Shit! Wouldn't you know?

We tried again, and got the same cry of pain from the winch. This was strange, because the winch had been handling other loads OK. So there must be a *huge* haul of black cod down there if the winch couldn't manage it, right?

I grabbed the radiophone and called Ron, a mechanic in Vancouver. My tone may have worried him. Something convinced him that this was no ordinary winch failure. It seemed to be an event of tragic dimensions. Ron said he could meet me in Gold River, the quickest place we could both get to — a six-hour boat trip for me and a seven-hour car trip for him, including a ferry ride over to Vancouver Island.

Leaving countless black cod trapped in the depths, I fought headwinds to Gold River. Ron was on the blustery dock, pacing to keep warm, a towering figure who looked like Gregory Peck playing Captain Ahab — except Ron had two sound legs, and had even set jogging records in our Porridge Club running group. He'd brought along a new winch pump, the same brand as the broken one. The hydraulic pump is what makes the winch go. Or *not* go, if it gets worn, starts to leak internally and can't handle great loads anymore.

The pump had to be installed in my engine room, a cranny already jammed and jutting with equipment. The pump had to go right up at the front, in a tight gap. It weighed two hundred pounds, and the work area suited a short and aerobic workman, not two large guys who could have been used by Central Casting as Viking foot soldiers.

With the jutting equipment and surprising places to stab ourselves and bang our knuckles, this project was as easy as working inside an Iron Maiden. The pump had to line up just so. We laboured and cursed the forces of evil until 2 a.m. At last Ron said it was OK. He yawned, ran up and down the dock to get his circulation going, got into his car and left.

I started the boat's engine and cast off. I steered directly into darkness, out the gusty channel from Gold River — a fiord a quarter of a mile wide. The crew were sleeping. I was alone, a valiant figure, speeding back to my tremendous catch of fish, the wind behind me this time. I wasn't daunted by the strenuous work or the lack of sleep. I had no concerns about future jinxes or battles.

I woke up with my head on my chest. I was slumped in my skipper's chair, with the boat steering itself on autopilot. Ahead I saw a spectre. The boat's searchlight lit up a giant tree. Trees don't grow in the channel, so I lurched and threw the engine into reverse. Less than three seconds went by, in horrifying slow motion, and the boat rammed the shoreline. And stopped. The impressive tree stood dead ahead. To the right and left, small but vigorous waves churned up gray pebbles.

Yes, I did have top-price electronics on that boat, including a vigilant radar and depth sounder. But nothing had been set to beep warnings.

The crew woke up. It was a hell of a crash. They sized up the situation and scooted around looking for holes in the bottom. There weren't any.

I managed to reverse off the shore, but found I couldn't steer. The rudder was stuck. I imagined it bent and jammed against the bottom of the boat. (It was a bendable piece of metal, if you hit it hard enough. These things happen.) I thought about the boat's stabilizers — designed to keep the craft from rolling too much in rough weather: they might serve to steer with. On each side of the boat there was a triangle of metal that could be run underwater like a little kite. These drags hung from the two trolling poles that reached out over the sides. We connected those triangle drags to the winch, so that when we pulled one drag closer to the hull, the other moved farther out. This gave more drag force on one side of the boat than the other. And that turned the boat. It worked well enough. And showed my brain was still OK.

This way I got the boat *back* into the little port at Gold River, where I had to wait for the citizens there to get out of bed at their normal hour. They informed me there wasn't any shipyard to haul the boat out.

Stuck. But one of my crew, Larry, had an idea. He'd been with me for two years and had a proven capacity to deal with crises. He was once a biker, still had long hair, only a few teeth, and an aggressive manner. Let me fill in a bit. He'd married an Indian girl at Port Alberni. On their honeymoon, she sighed to him that her kid brother Eddie was on skid row, a heroin addict. Larry responded in a can-do way. He located the severely drugged Eddie, yanked him to a cheap motel, and told him: "I'm cleaning you up!" He locked Eddie in the room. Larry brought the shaking addict food, and kept watch. Ten days passed and the treatment took. Eddie seemed cured, maybe because Larry had told him: "If you shoot heroin again, I'll shoot *you*." Eddie understood that Larry issued reliable warnings. But the therapy didn't stop there. Larry got Eddie a job, working alongside strong-willed Larry on a fishing boat. For some reason, ex-addict Eddie took to this seagoing life. He liked the tangy air, the squawk of sea birds, and even gutting the fish.

Now those two same guys were working for *me,* on my first fateful black-cod trip. Larry applied his can-do powers to fixing the wrecked rudder. He proposed mechanical first-aid: force the rudder back down by using the rudder's shaft. This seemed possible, so I said: "OK, try." (The shaft comes through the bottom of the boat and connects to hydraulic lines. Those lines turn the rudder, provided the rudder isn't crumpled against the underside of the boat.) As Larry and Eddie worked at this project, I could hear the familiar technical terms used in different stages of boat repair. "Fuck!" "What a bitch!"

They hammered together a rough timber frame, inside the boat right above the shaft, then used a hydraulic jack jammed against the frame to press down the rudder shaft. I knew something critical was happening when the cursing stopped. There was a solemn moment of silence. Then a sound like a rifle shot rang out — they'd freed it! At least I could now move it. And it worked, sort of. (Better than using the drags, which weren't good for long trips — too much total drag on the boat.)

With a rudder that probably looked like sheet-metal origami, we headed for Port Alberni, where I got a new rudder put in. Then I beat straight back to those trapped fish. Tons, tons, tons of them!

The GPS took us to a cluster of my fluoro-red buoys. We pulled up the anchor easily — the winch worked fine for that. So far, so good. Then we started to haul in the line of traps. The winch squealed again like a hernia victim. It didn't move the line at all.

I clutched my head. Ron had grumbled back in Gold River: "There must be a bypass valve somewhere in this damn circuit!" But we'd never found it. So I started following hydraulic lines now, like a crazed terrier. I wedged into every hole and angle, following the scent. When I arrived at a plywood panel behind the toilet, an instinct stopped me. I stared at the panel, with my ears pointed and my front paw lifted. Then I ripped at the plywood with a screwdriver and my bare hands. There it stood — a bypass valve. Such a convenient location! (Who designed this fucking boat?) A quarter turn on the valve, and the winch was fixed. That had been the problem all along. The only problem.

At last the traps came up. . . . There was only one or two pathetic black cod in each one. And not fat fish that had eaten the others. They were normal size, but half dead. The crew said nothing. Their solemn expressions might have suited a burial at sea. Their only pay was a percentage of the catch — after the boat expenses. But this trip had been *all* expenses — for fuel and grub. They'd later bitch among themselves, but not directly to me. (A seagoing courtesy to the skipper, from the days of keel-hauling.)

You'll be surprised to hear that I carried on with black cod fishing. You'll be surprised that the crew carried on. But we weren't normal humans. We were fishermen. Fishermen always think things will get better, even with the very next trap or hook. Or all we need is some minor adjustment in method. Or a better spot for the traps. There were plenty of places to try. It wasn't like the black-cod fishing regions were crowded with fishermen. Maybe some different bait? Anyway, Blair Pearl was out there catching tons of black cod, so it was possible.

I battled with the infernal traps for two months. It wasn't easier knowing that my buddies were lounging through sunny vacations in Hawaii and Mexico. They fished in summer for salmon and halibut. They didn't *consider* fishing in winter. But here I was in icy hurricanes, hauling up empty traps.

I had precisely one good day in two months. It was because of Earling (another quixotic black-cod fisherman with a small boat). He gave me a tip: ask the fish-processing plant near Bamfield for some of their rotten junk — heads, guts, tails. Then throw that stuff into the traps. Earling said he'd been doing it for a week and it worked "like magic." When I tried it and pulled up my traps, about 300 pounds of black cod were jammed into every one. The secret — black cod love *rotten* bait!

It never worked again. Later I found it was exactly wrong: black cod like *fresh* bait, not rotten. My first load of heads and tails must have been fairly fresh, purely by luck. That's why I'd had one sensational day.

The secret method stopped working for Earling too. For the record, because Earling may see this book, I want to say that I know the advice I got from him was well-meant. It wasn't typical for one skipper to tell another *anything* (remember my *Joy II* days, and all that lying?). So it was open and good-natured of Earling to tell me that secret, faulty as it was.

A year later, when much had changed, the skipper of a big trap boat filled me in, told me that Earling had really found part of the secret: "You guys should've thrown in half a dozen junk fish (but always *fresh* stuff), anything you can find or buy cheap — like hake. It's for the black cod to eat, while they're waiting for you to pull them up. So they don't eat each other. If you're lucky, it sets off a feeding frenzy inside the trap. That attracts lots of black cod into the trap."

The skipper picked up his whisky glass, and went on in a comradely way: "You can't be stingy with the bait, Eric! It's the natural oil in the bait that attracts them. The natural oil. Two days in the water, the bait loses the natural oil — useless." He was referring to the way I hardly put any bait in the little bait-bag that hangs in the centre of the trap. The smell of the bait diffuses out from there and attracts the fish. But I'd been using the same worn-out bait after we brought a trap up, after it had been a day or two in the water.

Even if I *had* known all that stuff, my boat was still too small. I could put down all my traps in six hours, and that wasn't enough time for many fish to get caught. I could have waited around, doing nothing, letting the traps fill up. Or bought more traps (if I could have afforded that and it had seemed like a good investment. Which it didn't, because I wasn't catching anything, no matter what I did).

In contrast, Blair was setting about 1,200 traps. He could turn over 400 of those a day, get to each trap every third day, and work his crew a 16-hour day — the sort of hours that guys *want* to work on a fishing boat. What else is there to do?

I gave up on traps. I was right to — even if I didn't know what I'd been doing wrong. But if I gave up on traps, I didn't give up on black cod. I knew that I could catch *some* black cod by long-lining, because I'd always pulled up a few while I was fishing for halibut. I speculated that by changing the depth, finding good spots, and using the right bait, long-lining could be made to work for black cod. I could use my everyday halibut gear. All I'd need was a smaller size of those new Norwegian circular hooks we'd been using.

While I was working this out, I experienced a great insight. It began suddenly, right after I made a sensational golf putt. It struck me that the insignificant haul of fish I caught in my traps had been sold to Canadian buyers. And they'd told me they shipped all their black cod to Japan. *Japan?* I finally wondered about that.

It got me asking around, and what I heard made my money-feelers tingle. It turned out the Japanese had known for hundreds of years that black cod have a special taste and texture because of their high oil content. That means unsmoked black cod is ideal for fast, high-heat cooking, exactly what the Japanese like to do. The cooked fish makes large, pure-white flakes, again ideal for their dishes.

Black cod used to cruise in great populations around Japan's northern coast. Way back, the Japanese wiped them out by overfishing. In the late 1960s, they started catching them off Alaska. In 1977 the U.S. 200-mile limit was declared, which should have blocked that. But it didn't, because Japan (and other foreigners) were allowed to fish inside 200 miles for species the host country *didn't* fish itself. So swarms of Japanese boats still roamed the Alaskan coastal waters, supposedly drag-fishing for dud species the Alaskans didn't want. That's what they said they were doing. They weren't allowed to target black cod, because some Alaskan boats did fish for those.

What the Japanese were really doing was fishing hard for black cod. Their seagoing factory ships would gut and clean the fish, freeze them, then take them straight to Japan. Who would know? They caught enough black cod off Alaska to supply the whole Japanese market — about 15,000 tons a year.

To prevent this sort of shenanigan, the far-sighted Americans had demanded an American observer on 1 percent of the Japanese boats, one picked at random every few days. But the boats that got the observers did everything by the strict (American) rule book. They'd ploddingly fish for junk fish, and stay away from their energetically poaching sister boats.

This hoodwinking went on for years. Then one Japanese boat was visited by a special foreign devil. The American observer who landed on their deck was new, and he spoke *Japanese*. No other observer ever had. He didn't let them know. He gazed at the sea, looking weary. But took in their radio talk. He must have ground his teeth, hearing how his boat was sent away from all the poachers in sight as soon as they found a good black-cod area.

The foreign devil wrote a vicious report to the American National Marine Service, which sent plainclothes observers to Japan. These experts lounged around the docks, telling cover stories to anyone who asked, and watched the poachers unload. When the Japanese met the Americans at the end of the year to negotiate for the next year's catch, the Japanese politely enquired what they were likely to be allowed to catch. They were told: You can't fish here *at all*. There was no saving face, or saving anything.

They couldn't fish for black cod outside the limit either, because black cod is all caught inside it. Outside the limit, it's too deep — often 6,000 feet, and nobody fishes that deep.

Japan had lost its source of illegal black cod. But the market in Japan needed to be filled. This was what Blair had found out, and what now spurred me.

Let me sum up the DFO situation on the day I gave up on traps. There was a generous black-cod quota of 5,000 tons a year. The quota had been set in the following scientific way: the DFO knew the Japanese had been fishing off Canada (before the 200-mile limit), and the Japanese said they'd been catching 5,000 tons a year. So that became the DFO quota! The black-cod season opened in February and closed in October. I don't know why they closed it, because the quota was never caught anyway.

When the fish were unloaded, any black-cod *buyer* had to tell DFO what they'd bought. If this figure ever accumulated to 5,000 tons before the season ended, then black-cod fishing would be stopped. But that never happened, because the total catch was limited by a more powerful mechanism: the low price for black cod.

The Cinderella fish

My switch to long-lining proved as easy as putting new sheets on a bunk. I stored the black-cod traps, probably pleasing a new group of spiders, and brought back my halibut gear.

I bought 7,000 circle hooks, taking a guess at the right size. I'd been using these circle hooks with powerful results for halibut (prompted by the Halibut Commission, which showed the hooks worked 30 percent better than normal hooks). This hook was the greatest invention I saw the whole time I was in long-line fishing. And remember, I started with *no* satellite navigation, *no* radiophones, nothing like that — but the circle hook was still the greatest advance. It looks like an ordinary hook that's been bent too far: the barb points back inward, toward the spine of the hook, as if trying to make a circle. When fish bite these hooks, they almost always get the hook in the corner of their mouths. That way they get hooked securely and it rarely pulls out. The strange thing is that I saw hooks just like that in my dad's shed, decades before the circle hook was "invented" in Norway. The hooks in the shed were roughly-made things, from sticks and rusty bits of steel. Dad said, "Old native hooks. For halibut."

So I had my new hooks, miles of old halibut line, my usual crew — all set. I picked out what seemed a good long-lining spot, where the continental shelf drops off suddenly. Along that precarious edge, peering at my fishfinder, I saw black cod moving around. They were deep. I couldn't think what else they might be.

I got the crew to bait the hooks with bits of squid — it has stiff rubbery flesh that stays on. (And I'd heard that black cod would eat anything.) I put down one line, an experiment, then hauled it up after four hours. I guessed it couldn't be left down there too long with that fresh squid on the hooks and lots of grotesque deep-sea life that probably wanted to eat it. Not to mention eat my hooked black cod.

The black-cod catch from that line turned out to be so-so. More black cod came up than I'd got using traps, for a similar effort. And that turned out to be typical. We'd grind away, pulling in lines of black cod, the catch was OK, but we never had any big days.

This way, the seasons passed. Not exactly merry and bright, but plodding away. We kept getting better at all this, and the trap boats also seemed to be getting better. Everyone was figuring things out.

We were a small group, we black-cod licence-holders, because the DFO had culled the licences in 1981. They'd seen something stirring in the black-cod fishery and decided it needed a slap of control. So they limited licences to boats that had fished black cod in the last two years. That left 48 boats, including the *Nordic Spirit*, which got a licence because those guys I bought it from had done enough black-cod fishing before they went broke.

Because Blair had the biggest boat, and I had one of the smallest, this generated a powerful static-electricity difference between our points of view. Enough to cause lightning storms. We argued about everything, but most of all about the fishing season. If the DFO opened the season in February, that was awful weather (as already noted), the fish were spawning in deep water, and a big boat like Blair's could get way out and fish on the spawning mass. Little boats like mine were lucky to get out of the goddamn harbour.

But if the season opened later, say in June, July or August, lots of the black cod would have moved to shallower banks to feed, they'd be more spread out, and perfect for long-lining. But *not* for Blair's trap fishing, because traps don't work well when the fish get shallower than 500 feet. (Maybe because their eyes can see the traps in the gloomy hue at that shallow depth.) This meant that Blair wouldn't do well in the summer, but I'd do real well. In short: *when* the season opened was critical to us both — and that divided the whole fleet, big boats versus little boats.

So we had berserk arguments. We'd lobby the DFO with the energy of environmentalists trying to save some species of frog. Both sides — big boats and little boats — felt sure the DFO had fallen under the malicious sway of the other side. Usually there was a truce and compromise. The season would open in May or April — a little late for big boats, a little early for boats like mine. But we could both manage.

Whatever season the DFO picked, we were all getting skilled enough so that we always caught more than the DFO quota. So they began cutting the seasons. (Sound familiar?) Meanwhile the price for black cod started rising. Every year prices would jump 30 percent, 40 percent — even 50 percent. There were reasons behind that perky rise. When the U.S. evicted the Japanese from Alaska, it meant the Japanese had lost their main black-cod source. At first they didn't trust the quality of Canadian black cod (for good reason), but as we got better, they started to believe we could deliver to their standard. But the DFO quota of 6,000 tons was fairly low — a lot less than the 15,000 tons the Japanese had been hauling out of Alaska — so the Japanese market was a vacuum. Anyway, we couldn't have caught 15,000 tons, even if our quota had been infinite. Up went the price.

In 1987, we created the Pacific Blackcod Fishermen's Association. The DFO was getting so heavy-handed that we wanted a common voice, rather than fighting back as individuals. This association wasn't easy to set up, because of the tension between big and little boats. Not everyone joined.

As the black-cod price rose, it pumped up our resolve to fish ever harder, which made the DFO wince. They cut us down to a two-month season. We worked harder in that shorter time. The fleet kept learning, keeping secrets from each other for a little while, but having them soon leak out. And everyone's technology and skills rose.

Our boats were like spacecraft that kept dropping into lower and faster orbits, as the seasons got shorter. What we lacked in fishing time, we made up in speed. We could imagine the DFO murmuring: "Those black-cod boats had two months last year and we'd set their quota at 5,000 tons, but they caught 6,000 tons. Next year, we'll only give them a month and a half." But we'd end up catching 7,000 tons! That went on until we were down to a whizzing orbit of 14 days of fishing a year.

Even the dimmest minds in the DFO began to understand this wasn't working. We overfished like mad for 14 days. It was havoc to the fish stocks. We must have swept above those black cod like a poisonous cloud. It was demented to haul in those fish in such big volume. It blew the quality, because of the rushed processing. We had to process and freeze them in two weeks. After that, Japan had a whole leisurely year to munch through them.

Out on the water, the black-cod fleet experienced a collective nervous breakdown. We couldn't take it. We were producing junk quality, overloading our boats, and losing traps (that went on fishing and then starved the black cod in those underwater gibbets). Boats sank. Guys drowned. So we were risking lives to catch fish that were there *all year*.

At last the big and little boats were united. It was like we came together under the banner, FUCK THIS.

My share is OK, your share is OK

In October 1989 I was president of the Pacific Blackcod Fish-ermen's Association (later we'd change the name from "black cod" to "sablefish" — the more up-market name for black cod). I called a special meeting to decide how to dish out an individual catch quota for each boat. I wasn't sure who'd come. Usually some guys stayed away. This time I told everyone they'd be nuts to miss it. I invited everyone with a black-cod licence, including standoffs who'd shunned the association totally (a couple of the big boats). I said they didn't have to be a member. Just come.

The meeting room filled. Everyone showed. Not because it was a new thing to talk about a quota system, but *doing* something about it was new. The idea had already been out there. Academics had written about it and proclaimed — as they tend to do — that This Is The Solution.

But we had to make the thing work out there on the wild water and at the docks.

Problem One: How to divide the yearly DFO black-cod quota among us fishermen. Everyone had a reason why they should get the bulk of it. Forty-eight guys had that compulsive opinion. Some of us had been hacking over this for months, in private. Whatever method we'd thought of to divide it up, someone else always wanted to change the formula a little, so they got a bit more. "Forget it. I want a fair share!"

At the big meeting we solved everything in about an hour. Blair started with a predictable sermon: The quota's got to be based on a boat's last five years of catch history (his catch was huge). And most guys were happy with that. But there were two boats as big as Blair's and they'd never caught much. They kept saying, almost chanting: No, no, no, no! It all has to be on the *size* of the boat! Big boats get more!

I'd foreseen this snag and had a compromise: base a boat's quota 70 percent on its catch history, averaged over the last three years (not five years), and 30 percent on the boat's size. Everyone liked that. Then another hand went up: Bobby Fraumeni (an inventive mind) said to the agitated group (the over-agitated group) that instead of averaging over the last three years, why not use the *best* year in the last three years? Cheers rose. Wonderful! No discussion. In a kind of hangover mood the next morning, I realized that group impulse had cost me about 20 percent of my quota. Moral: Don't agree to "obvious" mathematics in a hot-moving meeting.

Problem Two: We all worried that some guys might poach. We knew it was possible to catch our whole quota in two weeks (we'd been doing it). So that left a tempting span of time for poaching. How to police this? It didn't take long to solve: we'd hire a private security firm. They'd check the *landings* of black cod. Because if a boat couldn't land its fish, it wasn't in business. This seemed the way to handle it — not chase guys around on the water. (The DFO was already doing that, mainly for salmon, and not doing too well.)

Problem Three: Could we transfer our quotas around? Could we let one boat sell its quota to another boat? What about selling part of its quota? Some members worried: "We can't do it, the Japanese will buy the whole quota! We'll end up as slaves. Or big Canadian companies might buy it all." We assumed we were going to *own* the quota, which isn't quite what happened. A guy with a severe head cold and voice that consequently sounded like Darth Vader said: "Let's have some guts here. Make the quotas as transferable as they can be. Let anybody buy or sell. Just do it. See what happens. If it doesn't work, we can put restrictions on it later."

So we did that. And the Japanese never came in and bought *any* quota. No one was sure why, but I guess it was because the licensing system in Canada was pointlessly complicated, alien,

147

and the Japanese probably thought they'd be discriminated against. They were ending up with the whole catch in any case. So why bother?

The single black-cod licence that was already owned by a big Canadian fishing company was sold by them — immediately. They didn't see a future in black cod. Their profits were in salmon and herring. To them, fishing black cod was pathetic. Something to get out of, not *into*. They were glad to have the cash for the licence.

How the DFO received our prayer

OK, we were clear among ourselves — the association. What wasn't clear was how the DFO would take it. They were used to acting like God, controlling fishermen, setting quotas, deciding how little we could fish, then letting us scramble for it.

We had luck. The man at the DFO who managed black cod, Bruce Turris, had studied the academic work on individual boat quotas. He knew that we'd been talking about it, and he'd always seemed agreeable. A sensible DFO manager! Young, open-minded, he didn't see any reason why a structure couldn't be set up that let the black-cod fishermen run things. "You'll have to hire scientists," he told us, leaning forward with his aggressive playing-field shoulders. "You'll have to work out objectively how much black cod should be in the overall quota every year."

He pushed the association's quota plan into the terrifying wheelwork of the DFO approval system. Fortunately, all this happened at a fairly low level in the DFO. It got grabbed by the lower wheels only. At higher levels, the bigger wheels revolved around salmon, not some obscure fish like black cod, which good Canadians didn't even eat. (This was 1990.)

Time passed. Then the DFO consulted with the Sablefish Advisory Committee (SAC), an advisory panel of eight sablefish licence holders and a processing company — basically our own members! It's the eccentric way things worked. They created this exterior committee, just to approve things. The DFO felt insecure and must have sensed its incompetence in certain topics, so they sometimes did this kind of thing. That way they didn't have to shoulder full responsibility. This cover-butt system even applied to lowly black cod. Naturally, SAC said: Yeah, go for it! (Because SAC was a separate committee, but made up mainly of our association members — in case you're still having trouble believing this.) Protocol also required the proposal to be mailed to all black-cod licence holders, with a formal-looking ballot form.

Hey! Done! We had our quota system. And we'd be running it pretty much ourselves. It was what the DFO agreed to. This was new.

How the quotas work now

Individual boat quotas! The great ocean itself seemed changed. So much changed all at once, it seemed cosmic. But first let me speak narrowly, and for myself: *I* no longer felt *I* was trying to grab fish away from the other boats — on the principle that if I didn't get the fish, they would. Because I knew I could catch all that I was allowed to, in my sweet time.

But I felt anxious about poaching. What if some boat was out there secretly draining away the stocks? We'd set up our anti-poaching system, but we weren't too confident about it.

There was another immediate jolt: as a part claimant on the black cod out there, I felt suddenly motherly about them. I wanted them to thrive, and not take too many of them. I wanted to catch a little bit of black cod for the rest of my life, not wipe them out.

So I started resenting draggers. They caught black cod as by-catch. Those seemed like *my* fish. But I couldn't do anything. The association had to give 8 percent of the total black-cod catch to the drag fleet as by-catch, because the draggers had cried to the DFO they couldn't bring in their usual catches without pulling up some black cod. And another resentment smoldered: the draggers maul their black cod and turn it into junk. That damages the black-cod market. I still run into Canadian chefs who say, "Oh yeah, I tried black cod. Garbage! Never again!"

If I was bothered about the draggers, I was relieved about other things. Like making more profit. I was no longer frantic to make my boat a hyperactive killing machine — to grab more and more fish, in ever-shorter times. I now had plenty of time — almost all year. I saved on technological costs; we all did. And we all made more profit.

I could also schedule my fishing for the best market time. I didn't have to catch my quota in two weeks, freeze it and have someone put it in cold storage for months. (Japanese eat black cod mainly in the cold months of the year, so it's better to supply them at those times, which I now could.) Meanwhile the Alaskan black-cod fishermen were still madhouse fishing, cramming every-thing into a quick season. I could time my fishing to work *around* their supplies.

So everything became more easy-going. I could fish when I wanted to. The big boats could fish when they wanted to. Guys started helping each other, instead of acting like territorial rodents.

It meant the association was brightly transformed. Instead of grudging nominal dues of $100 a year, everyone contentedly kicked in much larger amounts — a percentage of the black-cod value they landed. Those dollars were used to pay our poaching police and to do research on the black-cod stocks (part of our agreement with the DFO).

The association had been meeting every three months, with a sulky low attendance. Now meetings became vital. We ap-pointed fifteen guys as directors (each represented about three boats). They had regular telephone conference calls to keep in touch and manage the daily business (which now had the tone of a co-operative). These phone conferences were just the thing, because we were spread out geographically. It's the way we still do it. (The old style of meeting in a big room still happens, but annually.)

How to intimidate poachers

Our security firm specializes in the fishing industry. Their people can tell a black cod from a herring, know the crafty minds of poachers, and monitor our fleet for deviant behaviour. They have officers in all the little fishing communities where people unload their catches.

This self-inflicted spy network presents the association with regular reports. Usually the reports are negative: where they'd been, what they'd monitored, and what *didn't* happen (no illegal black cod found). If any of their guys notice someone poaching, their job is to report it to us. We then flash the news to DFO enforcement personnel — fish cops, who move with the force of law. We even contribute to the DFO salaries and operating expenses for six of those fish cops, so they can spend part of their time on black-cod enforcement work. And they do cause a few thrills, like once *nearly* catching a dragger about to unload illegal black cod. As the cops got ready to storm the boat, the dragger started its thundering engines, took off and dumped the evidence in the bay.

These monitors and cops also poke their heads at random into the fish-processing plants, to see if anything improper is happening. The plants have to document where their fish come from, and show they bought them from a licensed boat.

All this surveillance costs us. The dockside monitoring program alone costs the association about $250,000 a year. But it's worked. For one thing, the black-cod quota for a boat is so valuable it's not worth cheating and risking losing it. The Minister has a right to cancel a fishing licence, but the only time he's done that is for poaching. A fearsome threat. A guy would have to poach on a scandalous scale to make that risk worthwhile. But big-time poaching just increases the risk, because boats need crews — and crews talk. The skipper can't secretly go out by himself and catch $2 million worth of black cod. And it takes time to catch fish, to clean them and pack them. More chance of getting spotted. It's not an operation that can be done in a few hours, in black night, wearing military night-vision goggles.

Because of those constraints and realities, our anti-poaching system works.

Pointing the scientists toward the fish

As soon as we considered the black cod as "our fish," we were dumbstruck at how little we knew about them. Not even roughly how many there might be out there, where they hang out, how they move around during their lives — even basics. (Remember, the DFO had been guessing when they set the yearly catch quota — using that outdated Japanese number of 5,000 tons, which was itself a rumour or lie.)

We talked to two DFO scientists who'd done a bit of work on black cod, part-time. We wanted them working for us. They agreed. We set up a grand-sounding Science Committee, with some guys from the association and those two scientists from the DFO. On the association side, we saw ourselves as amiable but ignorant fishermen. The DFO scientists came up with research projects and we'd ding like cash registers: "Great! Go for it! Here's the cash." Because these were *our* experts. Indeed they were.

We got expert and carefully written-up reports — about fairly weird questions. They pursued finicky scientific questions, mostly about ocean temperatures. For some reason, they loved analyzing ocean temperatures. And it wasn't as if they went around in boats and dipped thermometers in. They didn't *collect* data, they analyzed it. Some of the data they collected — picture this — was collected on trips to Russia. Our two DFO scientists went on many Russian junkets. Even as the DFO guys extracted this crucial data from the Russians, they bitched to them about their paltry budget and how it didn't allow them enough money to gather even more ocean-temperature data. (From congenial ocean scientists in what landlocked country, I wonder? Switzerland?)

This DFO love of Russia seemed to have uncanny resonances elsewhere in their organization. Certainly the whole place vibrated or droned according to the Soviet model of management philosophy. (Russia was still yoked to the strict Soviet system in those days.) The DFO staff never come from the coastal fishing communities. They all come from academic, urban communities. Some of them eventually rise to become DFO managers, clutching their biology or management degrees, gazing out of glass towers, and glaring at the untidy world through their severe Soviet-style wire-rimmed spectacles. And the Canadian Government *still* manages the nation's fish using the old Soviet model: they keep their senior management people 4,000 miles from the fish resource, manage it from Ottawa in a grand downtown building, with hundreds of comrades to help and keep up the ideology, all close to the massed ranks of main-chance politicians, who use the fish-management funds as a pork barrel. No connection with the fishing people on the coast, except to hurl instructions at them. And the Ottawa-Soviet model doesn't *consider* trying to make money for the industry. Not a criterion.

I get worked up thinking about that (this must be obvious). And those hot resentments were tumbling in my brain like clothes in a clothes dryer, while I sat there at one of our science committee meetings. Our two scientists were babbling about their ocean-temperature projects and the latest superior Russian data, while the rest of us wanted to get on with the business of our quota for next year. It was that time of year. We wanted to get the quota right, to protect our stocks.

Something fused in my brain, as if my clothes dryer had shorted out. I jabbed a finger at the scientists: "How many black cod are out there?" It had hit me that this was what we actually needed to know. The *main thing* we needed to know.

The scientists blinked and advised me they didn't know.

Then I said (my mental ocean-temperature rising): "Then how the hell would you find out?"

One of them advised: "Well, we would need to tag a sufficient number of fish and determine how many are returned in the subsequent catches."

They were honest enough to admit they didn't have any estimate of how many fish were out there. Because they hadn't been asking that question. I saw that we hadn't been getting our money's worth. They'd been doing these fastidious and pointless projects for three years. Not only did they not have any notion of the mass of fish out there, they had never thought about it.

I said, levelling my increasing understanding of science at them: "How come we aren't doing that tagging right now?"

One of them, the more talkative, said: "We carried out a study like that ten years ago, for two years. However, we expended the small budget and were forced to terminate it. The project had been too short to reach a meaningful conclusion."

So tagging would be fine, according to them, given enough money and time. But I didn't trust them. My trust in their ocean-temperature work had declined over three years, at least subconsciously. Tumble, tumble, tumble went my brain, working away. Before today, I hadn't built up much confidence in my own hunches. (Those scientists must know what they're doing!) Meanwhile, I'd started a kind of astral-plane search for a second opinion. It happened smoothly, because I was elected head of the Halibut Fishermen's Association around that time (early 1980s), and I was going to all their meetings. So when this tagging idea came up, I had a top contact: the head of the Halibut Commission, a buddy. Did he know any fish scientist who might be clued-in about black cod?

He suggested three. One was Ray Hilborn, professor of aquatic and fishery sciences at the University of Washington. I was told that Ray was a world-class researcher, and even did projects for fishermen in New Zealand and Australia. I remembered meeting Ray at a conference maybe ten years before — a strong-voiced, outgoing guy, and a polished communicator. He could put things simply to us fishermen — even a maze of numbers and logic, like population statistics for biological systems. I also happened to have a friend who was renting Ray's house in Vancouver. (Ray is Canadian, but lives in the U.S.) So I felt a kind of fateful astral connection to this scientist. Not to say trust.

I phoned Ray, told him my qualms about our ocean-temperature addicts, and said we might be looking for outside scientific help. And I put the idea of the tagging to him. *"Absolutely,"* he responded. Tagging was what we needed. And he'd help.

Black cod with noodles

Ray worked out a tagging program for us, and we got it going. We tagged about 20,000 black cod the first year, and continued in the following years.

The tags look like a spaghetti noodle that's made of plastic, except they're an unnaturally bright yellow. At one end, there's a little plastic hook. That gets hooked into the back of the fish, through the skin and right into the meat. It heals up, and the fish tows along this low-drag noodle, with no problems. (It's like one of their normal parasites, a leech that black cod sometimes get anyway, and can cope with fine).

Each tag has a number on it. I mean an actual number, not a bar code. That means the numbers are a bit hard to see, considering they're written on a noodle. (But they can be read by lab guys with youthful eyeballs, or optical aids.)

One of our association boats is hired to do the tagging work. The skipper gets paid, and also compensated for the black cod that are tagged (and normally would have been kept and sold). There's the usual crew on board to trap the black cod, and a couple of guys from a scientific consultancy (most often new university graduates, in their first field job). The skipper follows instructions on printouts supplied by our tagging scientist, Ray. The tagging is always done from the same spots, year after year — at selected places along the coast — so we can later work out what happens in each spot, over a long period.

So picture this tagging boat, cruising up and down the coast, trap-fishing black cod from certain exact locations. A percentage of the black cod brought up in the traps are tagged, their lengths are measured and they're weighed. (It would be handy to record their ages too, but that's not possible: the fish would have to be killed and a piece of their ear-bone taken out and examined.) Then the tagged fish are thrown back in, now distinct with their yellow spaghetti noodle, and they mix with the rest down there.

We get the tagged fish back when (or if) someone catches them in the normal way. Fishermen that catch a tagged black cod might not be members of our association. They might not even be Canadians. Fishermen from Alaska have caught some. So why would they bother to tell us? Why not take off the tag and sell the fish?

Reason: Any fisherman who catches a tagged black cod knows there's an incentive to turn it in.

We also advertise prizes in fishing magazines. Word gets around. For a few tags, we give them a hat! (Sounds funny or maybe cheapskate, but the guys like the hats.) For every 20 tags, they get a jacket — a good-quality sporty one. There are also golf shirts, not to mention a lottery that can be won by turning in even one tagged black cod. Turn in the lucky fish and win a trip to Mexico!

They only have to freeze all the tagged fish and keep them separate. When those fish get to the tagging scientists (our consultants again, but sometimes the DFO handles part of the lab work), they have a close look at each fish, reweigh it and measure it. And also check its age. All this gives us data about growth rates and some information about migrations (tagged fish can take years to come in, and the fish may have wandered a long way).

Meanwhile we have another data-collection program going on, also designed by Ray. Each association fisherman is required to hand in a certain number of black cod a year for biological inspection. These fish are given a real go-over: age, sex, maturity, and stomach contents are recorded. It's a random-sampling system: a printout might tell the boat's skipper to take the fifth trap on the fourth string in a certain area.

But it's not the biological data that give the crucial information for calculating the stocks. It's those tagged fish we get back. The rough idea is this: the tagged black cod mix with the rest of the black cod, and if we catch 5 percent of the tagged fish, then we assume that we're catching 5 percent of the whole black-cod population.

Unlike the salmon fishermen who catch up to 70 percent of the salmon stock, we catch only 10 percent of the black-cod stock every year.

But refinements are needed to make good sense of the tag counts. Tags come in from different years. Some tagged fish die or get eaten by predators, and never show up. Others take ten years to get back, and all this has to be modelled with mathematical finesse. It takes sophisticated analysis, with all these layers of effects and cross-currents of data. Ray broods over the data.

I started with the impression that tagging would tell us exactly what was happening in the depths. I've found it does that to *some* degree, but raises a cloud of questions. Like: Why do all the tagged fish disappear for a year or so, then show up? That seemed to say in our first tagging years that we were catching zero percent of the stock! Ray had warned us that might happen, and calmed us down. He still isn't exactly sure why the black cod behave like that. Maybe they're upset by tagging, and they're wary of traps for a while. Anyway, we start catching them again in about the third year, and they come in for years afterwards.

Other valuable or peculiar facts emerge. For example, why didn't we get any black cod back that were caught in very deep water and tagged? It took a while to work out. We tried putting a few tagged fish back in the traps and sending them down again. When we brought these same experimental fish back up once more, they were always *dead*. Our lab got on the case. A blood test of the victims showed that they'd got the bends coming up. We pulled them up fast, so their blood fizzed. Just like human deep-sea divers. This led to a system for tagging fish in deep water: we simply haul them up slowly.

That info on bends was useful, if depressing. It meant that when draggers brought up their black-cod by-catch, then threw back the small ones, those fish would all die. And draggers work very deep these days — sometimes down to 5,000 feet, because they've dragged out all the shallow grounds. That hurts our stocks.

This is the kind of stuff we're learning. Not perfect, but useful.

(A lot more useful than finding out about ocean temperatures from Russians.) But you might think: isn't there some easier way? Why not lower a camera and watch the black cod on a screen? Well, no. It's deep where these fish live, and it's black. We'd have to put down lights, and that would change their environment — chase them away, or attract them. Second, we'd only be sampling a tiny area.

One thing could give better data: satellite tags. It's done with tropical tuna, for example — big fish that weigh 1,500 pounds. Technicians can attach a data-pod to a tuna. The pod monitors the water temperature, depth and light intensity. When the pod's battery is about to run out, the pod detaches and floats to the surface, then beams up the stored information to a satellite. The light-intensity data is converted to a measure of latitude and longitude, so the tuna's path can be worked out. The beauty is that you don't have to *catch* the fish to get the data. But we can't do that for black cod: the pods are too big (so far), and each one is too expensive — a couple of thousand dollars. It's OK for tuna, because it's such a big fish and so valuable (typically worth $20,000 each).

Fish come in waves

In 2001, we were bewildered and panicked. Our black-cod catch was collapsing. All year our fishing had been crap.

Soon we saw that this was a natural cycle. I knew that the crab population varies by a factor of 100, and rises and falls according to a 20-year cycle. Also, there were times in the past when I'd catch 1,500 pounds of halibut on a single line. A decade later I'd catch 15,000 pounds in the same place. Then it would decline again. In marine populations, there are always cycles. There's that plain connection between predators and their prey. Fish feed on other creatures, in a Great Chain of Being right down to plankton. If one species varies in numbers, even by chance, all the rest have to vary. If one type of fish declines, then fish that feed on it soon decline. When the bottom species recovers (because its predators have been starved back to very low numbers), the bottom species comes back fast and even overshoots a long way. Up and down go all the numbers, over great spans of years. Interlocking dependency, cycles within cycles, and all quite natural and stable over a long enough view.

We could even see our future black-cod stock coming back, once we'd stepped back from our panic. We saw a great mass of juveniles coming out of the fiords. Everyone was catching them and throwing them back. They had disappeared out to deep water, and were too small for us to catch. (I'll tell you why in a second.) Those young will come back as new stock, but that surge is about five years away. Meanwhile, it all looked exactly like a natural cycle, and we could see that in our long-term log data. We were just getting to a normal low for the black-cod cycle. No need to panic.

Knowing that, the association pushed for a gross reduction in our quotas. It was responsible. And think: We were the first to discover this black-cod cycle, and we immediately acted on it. It was a pre-emptive act — a model of how fish stocks *should* be handled.

Escape holes

Trap-boat skippers had always been perturbed about the baby black cod they caught. The tunnel size in the traps had been calculated *not* to catch much *except* black cod, but they still caught baby black cod. They were thrown back, of course. (Most would have survived OK, because our boats weren't fishing in such deep water then, so the babies wouldn't have had gotten bends.) But dolphins found out about these juvenile tidbits that were going over the side. They ate the little black cod. It was as if the dolphins heard about a new gourmet restaurant opening — news got around that fast.

One of our inventive people suggested putting escape holes in the traps — big enough for the babies to get out, but small enough to keep other black cod in. But a self-important DFO scientist laid down the law: "We already examined that. We carried out a study nine years ago." If he had worn a monocle, he would have adjusted it at this point, or polished it. Instead he sniffed and said: "That study proved inconclusive."

In case you're wondering: Why had the DFO done research on a fish all those years ago, back when no one had any commercial interest in it? Simple. It was *because* no one had any interest. A perfect science project! An exotic, forgotten, useless fish. No commercial value. What could be more ideal? The researchers would be left alone. No one would care if they got nowhere and stopped.

But our inventor Bobby Fraumeni was too worked up about the dolphins to give up. He even had a tank of seawater on deck, where he kept the little ones alive and then dumped them all at once — hoping that most might escape the dolphins in the scramble and confusion.

Bobby built experimental traps with escape holes, muttering in the manner of Galileo, "Fuck that DFO know-it-all." Bobby didn't say much to us. But he could be seen out in his boat, lowering traps, bringing them in, then lowering them again.

Then I had a call from him. "It works!" he said.

"Is this secret?" I wanted to know.

"No, no!" he said. "I'm telling everyone. We've got to do it! All the little ones get out, and more big ones get in — because there's more space."

He drew diagrams and wrote a couple of pages about what he'd done — the size of the metal rings he'd used to make permanent escape holes in the trap walls, how he fastened them into the net, and how to contact the manufacturer that would make the rings on order. He faxed a copy to every fisherman in the association. In less than three weeks, all the trap boats were doing it.

At the next science committee meeting, we presented this news to a DFO scientist. We told him we wanted escape holes as a DFO *requirement* for black-cod traps. He made warding-off gestures, as if bothered by a fly: "It wasn't a correct scientific study that Bobby Fraumeni carried out. We need to replicate it properly."

So we said: "Right! We'll pay for it."

The DFO put two technicians on Bobby's boat, and they noted what happened with traps that had different sizes of escape holes. And they agreed that the right size of hole worked. When they wrote up a paper about it, in the customary dehydrated DFO style, it was published in some journal. That way it became official, and was elevated to a rule of the association in 1999: "All 'K' licensed vessels using traps to capture sablefish must have at least two escape openings in the side walls of each trap. The escape openings must have an inside diameter of at least 3.5 inches (8.89 cm), and are necessary to minimize the capture and mortality of juvenile sablefish. The escape opening requirement will be included in the 2000/2001 Sablefish Conditions of License (section 3.3.)."

Our inventor Bobby has turned to another challenge: how to stop big females from getting into the traps — the females that are fat and laden with spawn. (DFO: Watch this space.)

"The Institute of Advanced Black Cod Studies"

Our research has powered along for a decade. I'm proud of it. We fishermen never thought we could contribute, except by paying research costs. It seems such an unlikely thing, these fishermen with no former interest in such matters, now closely quizzing top scientists and demanding to understand the details. All this excitement of the chase . . . about science.

We feel sure there'll be breakthroughs. Black cod are still a mystery. Everywhere we've fished, there are scattered black cod. Sometimes they're small but shockingly old. Some are 30 years old, the lab tells us — but only weigh two pounds. Normally black cod weigh about eight pounds. What have these ancient and withered fish been doing? And if it's true that the whole seabed from Canada to Hawaii has scattered black cod, that's a gigantic stock. Maybe we've got fifty times more black cod than we thought. So if we took more than we do from the coastal waters, might others come up from the rich unknown beyond the continental shelf, grow fat, and take their place? Or don't those things connect? We haven't looked at DNA comparisons either, and mapped out the subspecies. It all gives me the feeling that fish science is about where medicine was in the seventeenth century when Dr. William Harvey was boggled to find that blood circulates. Much more to be learned.

We're already looking ahead to ocean ranching. Somehow helping the big spawners, and doing what we can to get more babies back out there. We've been talking about putting research money aside.

Summing up

When the DFO managed the black-cod fishery by itself, it reduced the fishermen to operators of isolated and belligerently competing boats. All against all. No energy or money went into useful science or was devoted to the quality of black cod that was shipped out of Canada. When the black-cod season fell to 14 days, we saw that the system wasn't working for anybody. We were squabbling, boats were sinking, guys were drowning, and we were landing poor-quality fish — because the work was so rushed. We overfished the "quota" every year, and no one was really managing the stock. *The DFO knew nothing about the stock.* We didn't either.

The fishermen put aside their feuds, and gathered in a room to plan something better. We reached agreement on individual quotas, and the DFO said OK. Now the Canadian Sablefish Association and the DFO seem to share the same aim — the proper care and management of the black-cod resource. The association truly does have that aim, and the DFO *says* it has. The DFO got itself into this black-cod quota system only because we pushed them. Now they're stuck with it. (Another example of the timeless principle that almost anything is easier to get into than get out of.) There *are* DFO people who push for quotas in a few other fisheries. But most DFO staff don't.

The DFO seems to view individual boat quotas and management by fishermen as giving up the DFO's near-hereditary powers. And that's right. I sense they don't give a damn about the best way to manage fishing. Everything is about their power. How do I know? I've had so many meetings with them, I'd be blind and deaf not to pick it up. Their outlook is so different, they talk right past the fishermen. People who go to work for the DFO go there partly for security. They won't ever have the feeling of pulling up to a dock with a $100,000 catch, but they get a safe wage, some sense of importance, paid holidays, and other goodies. But out on the ocean, fishermen can bring in riches, or meet abrupt ruin. The gods can capsize your little boat at a whim, and turn you into a sodden corpse. Nemesis watches you all the time.

With even more sweep ...

In BC, the people of Canada spend about $300 million to manage the fisheries. $100 million-plus of that goes to the collapsed salmon fishery, which doesn't produce more than about

$50 million worth of fish. Salmon used to produce $400 million worth of fish. Compare that collapse with black cod, and the responsibility the black-cod fishermen show for their stocks.

If the DFO really wanted well-managed fisheries, they'd give Canadian fishermen what Australian and New Zealand fishermen already have: property rights over the fish stocks. In Japan the fishing communities own the wild and farmed fish stocks, and operate them very successfully. With Canadian government "ownership" of the fish, the bureaucrats look after themselves and the fish get destroyed. If there were private ownership, the owners would look after the fish. Just like people who own their own houses and businesses look after them — indeed, cherish them. Simple human nature.

Is this radical or hard to understand?

8

Epilogue

*Teiresias bade me travel far and wide, carrying
an oar, till I came to a country where the people
have never heard of the sea, and do not even mix
salt with their food. They know nothing about
ships, nor oars that are as the wings of a ship. He
gave me this certain token which I will not hide
from you. He said that a wayfarer should meet me
and ask me whether it was a winnowing shovel
that I had on my shoulder. On this, I was to fix my
oar in the ground and sacrifice a ram, a bull, and
a boar to Neptune; after which I was to go home
and offer hecatombs to all the gods in heaven, one
after the other. As for myself, he said that death
should come to me from the sea, and that my life
should ebb away very gently when I was full of
years and peace of mind, and my people should
bless me.*

Homer, *The Odyssey*

So far, so good.

I've travelled about as far as I can from Canada. And I can't see
the sea, or smell it, where I live in Australia. I haven't tried carrying an oar to see if a wayfarer mistakes it for a shovel, but in a

way I *converted* my oar to a shovel: I bought land and planted a bunch of olive trees. A grove. Homer would have relished that.

I don't yet feel "full of years," but the hourglass does run faster. And maybe more ominously, my peace of mind is gaining strength.

I've now done everything I can. For decades, I struggled against the DFO in politically correct ways, through committees and fishermen's groups. In the end, it seemed in vain. Shoals of DFO employees still drift through the days in their giant glass towers, and may even breed there, like pampered fish in aquariums. They spend $1.3 billion a year managing a fishing industry that hardly exists anymore. Meanwhile, desolation washes the old fishing villages. Fifty-five thousand jobs lost in Canada, while DFO staff numbers stand at a new high of over 6,000.

Canadians are mostly convinced by the well-funded PR from the DFO, such as the recent DFO announcement that the salmon run on the Fraser was likely to double next year. From three million fish to six million! Wow. What they don't mention is the Fraser has spawning room for 100 million fish. Six million fish is just as pathetic as three million.

Here's a fact: Every major fishery the DFO ever managed has collapsed. But the two fisheries it *hasn't* managed — black cod and halibut — both thrive. I know about those surviving fisheries, because I'm still connected to them, by a single fishing line: Bobby Fraumeni and I are partners. I'm the partner who can no longer bear 18-hour days or summon enough athletic strength. Bobby has the young blood, and runs a Canadian boat that is partly mine. (He runs three other boats too, and has about 30 guys working for him.)

I am still a member of the black-cod association (now the Canadian Sablefish Association). They include me in their conference calls, I keep up with where we are in the black-cod cycle, read the scientific reports, and spend some time each year in Canada with the guys. And visit my expanding universe of kinfolk.

While I was writing these last pages, Bobby phoned. "You know, Eric, no one's built any boats in the last 15 years."

It's another one of those gradually deteriorating things that suddenly snaps your brain to attention when you notice. The boats are disappearing. Canadian fishing boats are being sold off overseas, and all the little shipyards have closed.

This means that even if Canada wanted to rebuild its coastal fishing communities (some chance!), there are no fishermen left, or mainly ageing ones, and no one will even be able to *build* boats anymore. Bamfield is a place for city tourists; it sparkles with holiday cottages. The few fishing people who live there are as time-worn as the broken boats that can sometimes be found in old coastal washes.

But now night comes to the village, and all along the coast. And the old ones sleep, and dream.

> *So we made fast the braces, took our thwarts,*
> *and let the wind and steersman work the ship*
> *with full sail spread all day above our coursing,*
> *till the sun dipped, and all the ways grew dark*
> *upon the fathomless unresting sea.*

Homer, *The Odyssey*

About the author

Eric Wickham was born in the small BC coastal village of Bamfield in 1942. For fifty years he was active in BC's fishing industry as a commercial fisherman and as an advocate for commercial fishermen in their struggle with the federal government. He is past president of the Pacific Blackcod Association, the Fishermen's Abalone Association and the Halibut Fishermen's Association, and is a past member of the Ministry of Fisheries' Advisory Council. Now retired and living in Western Australia, he returns to British Columbia annually.